Do Better. Be Better.

Shay Herbord

Published by Shay Herbord, 2024.

Table of Contents

Chapter 1: Motivation

Motivation, the driving force behind our actions and ambitions, often seems elusive, leaving many of us wondering why it's so challenging to summon at will. Understanding the intricacies of human motivation requires us to delve into the psychology of behavior, uncovering the reasons behind our resistance to change and the allure of inertia.

At the core of the struggle lies the intricate interplay between comfort and discomfort. Humans are creatures of habit, seeking the path of least resistance to preserve energy and maintain a sense of security. This inclination towards the familiar creates a comfort zone that, while providing solace, can also become a breeding ground for complacency. It is within this comfort zone that the specter of laziness often lurks.

Laziness and Fear of Change

Laziness, often dismissed as a simple lack of motivation or willpower, is a complex aspect of human behavior with multifaceted implications. Understanding its roots, its universal impact, and its exacerbation in the contemporary hustle and bustle is crucial for comprehending its pervasive influence.

Laziness, fundamentally, is a behavioral inclination rooted in the human tendency to conserve energy. Evolutionarily, conserving energy was a survival strategy when resources were scarce. Consequently, the human brain is wired to prioritize efficiency and reduce unnecessary exertion. While this inclination served our ancestors well in times of scarcity, the modern world presents a surplus of stimuli, making it challenging to distinguish between necessary and expendable efforts.

The impact of laziness is universal, affecting individuals across diverse backgrounds and contexts. It manifests not only as a reluctance to engage in physical activities but also as a resistance to mental exertion, change, or anything that disrupts the familiar. This universality stems from the shared human experience of seeking comfort and avoiding discomfort, a trait ingrained in our evolutionary history.

Moreover, laziness has a ripple effect on various aspects of life, including personal growth, professional development, and interpersonal relationships. It can hinder progress and innovation, preventing individuals from reaching their full potential and stifling creativity.

In the contemporary world, the prevalence of laziness is exacerbated by the constant influx of information, stimuli, and the demands of daily life. The fast-paced nature of modern society, coupled with the omnipresence of technology, introduces a paradoxical situation. While advancements are designed to make life more efficient, they also contribute to information overload and an overwhelming array of choices, leading to decision fatigue.

The perpetual bombardment of tasks, notifications, and responsibilities contributes to a sense of overwhelm. In response, individuals may default to a state of inertia, a form of coping mechanism against the incessant demands on their cognitive and physical resources.

Understanding the dynamics of laziness in this context is vital for developing strategies to counter its effects. By fostering self-awareness, implementing effective time management, and cultivating a mindful approach to daily challenges, individuals can navigate the complexities of modern life and mitigate the impact of laziness on their overall well-being and success.

The fear of change is a powerful force that can significantly impact an individual's motivation. This fear often originates from a discomfort with the unknown. Humans are creatures of habit, and stepping outside the familiar comfort zone can evoke a sense of vulnerability. The reluctance to leave this comfort zone contributes to a state of inertia, where individuals resist new opportunities and challenges.

Moreover, the fear of change is closely linked to a fear of failure. The potential consequences of change, whether they involve personal relationships or professional endeavors, can be daunting. This fear of the unknown consequences can paralyze individuals, preventing them from taking the necessary steps toward growth and improvement.

In the modern context, where change is a constant in both personal and professional spheres, the fear of change can become particularly pronounced. The fast-paced nature of contemporary life, coupled with the constant influx of information and stimuli, can create a sense of overwhelm. In response to this overload, individuals may retreat into a state of inertia, further intensifying the fear of change.

<u>What Motivates You Vs What Doesn't</u>

Motivation is a deeply personal and multifaceted aspect of the human experience, driven by a myriad of factors that vary from individual to individual. Understanding what motivates humans requires recognizing the diversity of aspirations, values, and connections that shape our pursuits. The essence of motivation lies in the alignment of goals with personal values and desires. Each person carries a unique set of values and experiences, forged through cultural background, upbringing, personal interests, and past successes or failures. These factors contribute to a complex tapestry that shapes individual motivations.

Connection plays a pivotal role in the motivational landscape. When individuals feel a personal and emotional connection to a goal, task, or outcome, motivation tends to flourish. This connection can stem from a variety of sources—personal interests, passions, relationships, or a sense of purpose. When something resonates with an individual on a deeper level, it becomes a driving force that propels them forward.

Conversely, motivation often wanes when individuals encounter tasks or goals that lack personal significance or relevance. The absence of a meaningful connection creates a gap between the individual and the objective, making it challenging to summon the drive necessary for sustained effort. This is why tasks perceived as mundane, irrelevant, or imposed from external sources can be particularly difficult to tackle with enthusiasm.

An example of this is something we see in children. The reason children have a harder time focusing and doing things at a younger age is due to the connection. Children who are told to learn simple math strictly and logically will eventually learn it, but it is like fighting an uphill battle. If you instead make learning math fun and something they can relate to, it makes the child more engaged and motivated to learn. This is why children are taught to sing the ABCs and simple games that help them learn while simulating as if they were merely playing a normal care-free game.

The concept of autonomy further underscores the importance of personal connection in motivation. When individuals have a sense of control and choice over their pursuits, motivation tends to be more robust. Autonomy allows individuals to align their goals with their values and preferences, fostering a deeper connection and a greater likelihood of sustained effort.

In essence, the diversity in what motivates humans is a testament to the rich tapestry of human experience. Whether driven by personal passions, a sense of purpose, or the pursuit of meaningful connections, motivations are inherently intertwined with individual identity. Recognizing and fostering these connections is key to unlocking sustained motivation, as it transforms the pursuit of goals from a chore into a meaningful and fulfilling journey.

The key to all of this is to find that connection to what you wish to be motivated about. Whether it is as simple as a small task or as large as a dream, making that connection helps feel like you are working towards something you yearn for.

<u>The Carrot and the Stick</u>

The concept of "the carrot and the stick" represents a time-tested approach to motivation, encompassing both reward-driven and consequence-based strategies. This metaphorical duo illustrates the idea that individuals can be motivated by the promise of a reward (the carrot) or the threat of consequences (the stick). Understanding and leveraging these motivational techniques can be instrumental in enhancing productivity and achieving personal or professional goals.

The Carrot: Rewards and Positive Reinforcement

"The carrot" signifies the use of rewards or positive reinforcement to motivate individuals. This approach involves offering incentives, recognition, or tangible benefits as a means of encouraging desired behavior or task completion. Rewards can take various forms, such as financial bonuses, praise, promotions, or even personal gratification.

The psychology behind the carrot lies in the positive association created between the task and the subsequent reward. This positive reinforcement reinforces the behavior, making individuals more inclined to repeat it. The anticipation of a reward serves as a powerful motivator, tapping into the pleasure centers of the brain and fostering a sense of accomplishment. The best thing to do is to link something that is a reward that you either want or that connects to the thing you wish to be motivated for. For example, if you are trying to learn a new language and are doing well, get yourself a gift or go out to eat linked to the language you are learning. Rewards don't have to be big, but the better the reward the higher the chance of success of completing the task.

The Stick: Consequences and Discipline

Conversely, "the stick" represents consequence-based motivation, where individuals are driven by the fear of negative outcomes or penalties. This approach involves setting boundaries, enforcing strict guidelines, or imposing consequences for failing to meet expectations. These consequences may include loss of privileges, missed opportunities, or other forms of discipline.

The stick strategy relies on the avoidance of negative consequences as a motivator. The fear of facing adverse outcomes can be a compelling force, prompting individuals to adhere to expectations and stay focused on their tasks. The imposition of discipline, while not as immediately gratifying as rewards, can instill a sense of accountability and urgency. This is one many people can relate to growing up. A parent or adult might have told you to do something so that you may not lose a privilege like watching TV or playing a game.

It is harder for adults to set this upon themselves when you can at any time reinstate the loss of privilege. A good suggestion is having an accountabili-buddy. This is a person who can help make sure you are staying motivated and can initiate and enforce the stick without you being able to reinstate the lost privilege. An interesting thing that might help is if another individual is also trying to motivate themselves to do so. By being another person's accountabili-buddy, you can ensure they continue to be motivated and they will hold you accountable also.

Balancing the Carrot and the Stick for Optimal Motivation

Effectively harnessing motivation often involves a balanced approach, recognizing that different situations and individuals may respond better to either the carrot or the stick. Striking the right balance requires understanding the nature of the task, the preferences of the individual, and the desired outcomes.

For tasks that align with personal interests or values, the carrot may be particularly effective. On the other hand, when facing distractions or tasks that demand discipline, the stick may provide the necessary structure and accountability.

Ultimately, the carrot and the stick represent complementary tools in the motivational toolbox. Recognizing when to apply each strategy can empower individuals to navigate the challenges of motivation, enhancing their ability to achieve goals and maintain focus on the tasks at hand.

<u>**Motivation and its Influence**</u>

Motivation, akin to an infectious spark, possesses an extraordinary capability to diffuse its energy and influence seamlessly from one person to the next. Witnessing an individual driven and passionate about tackling a challenging task serves as a potent catalyst, instigating inspiration in those who observe. This phenomenon underscores the contagious essence of motivation and its capacity to generate a positive ripple effect.

Observational learning is at the heart of this infectious nature of motivation. The demonstration of someone successfully confronting a demanding task with enthusiasm and dedication not only sparks a sense of possibility but also serves as a model for effective strategies and behaviors. This observation provides a tangible example of what is achievable, inspiring a collective belief in the attainability of difficult tasks.

Moreover, motivation, often accompanied by a positive emotional state, is subject to emotional contagion. When individuals express genuine passion, determination, or joy in pursuing a challenging goal, those around them are prone to catching that enthusiasm. This emotional contagion creates a shared positive atmosphere, fostering a collective sense of confidence in the face of challenging endeavors. The infectious quality of motivation is particularly pronounced within community or group settings. Members witnessing each other's commitment and perseverance creates a sense of camaraderie and mutual support. The shared pursuit of challenging goals establishes a positive feedback loop, where each individual's efforts contribute to the motivation of the entire group.

Achievement of challenging tasks by motivated individuals serves as living proof of what dedication and effort can yield. Witnessing someone overcome obstacles and achieve success inspires others to believe in their own capabilities and undertake similar challenges. This demonstration of achievement becomes a powerful source of motivation, igniting a desire for personal growth and accomplishment.

Leaders and influencers, embodying motivation, play a pivotal role in its infectious nature. Whether in professional settings, community initiatives, or personal relationships, leaders who exude passion and dedication inspire those around them to adopt a similar mindset. This influence extends beyond words; actions and genuine commitment become compelling sources of inspiration.

The infectious quality of motivation creates positive feedback loops within social circles. As one person's motivation encourages others to take on challenges, the collective achievements of the group further fuel the motivation of each individual. This cyclical process contributes to a culture of continuous improvement and shared enthusiasm. In this way, motivation transcends individual efforts, becoming a collective force that transforms challenges into shared opportunities for growth and achievement.

Motivation in a Society

Motivation, as a driving force within individuals and societies, plays a pivotal role in shaping the trajectory of humankind. At its core, motivation propels individuals toward action, and when aggregated at a societal level, it becomes a powerful engine that propels entire civilizations forward. Societal progress, economic development, cultural and artistic achievements, social change, and global collaboration are all manifestations of the profound impact of motivation on the human experience.

The collective aspirations and ambitions of individuals, driven by their motivations, contribute to the advancement of societies. The pursuit of knowledge, technological innovation, and the desire for societal betterment are all fueled by a shared motivation to reach higher standards of living and understanding. In the economic realm, motivation is a key driver of productivity and growth. Entrepreneurial ventures, technological breakthroughs, and advancements in various industries are often fueled by the motivation to succeed, compete, and innovate. The relentless pursuit of economic prosperity is deeply ingrained in the human spirit and has propelled societies to unprecedented levels of development.

Motivation is not solely confined to practical or economic pursuits; it is also a driving force behind cultural and artistic achievements. The motivation to express oneself, create beauty, and leave a lasting legacy has given rise to great works of art, literature, music, and scientific discoveries. These cultural and intellectual advancements contribute to the richness and diversity of human civilization.

Motivation has played a crucial role in movements for social change and justice. The desire to rectify societal inequalities, fight for human rights, and challenge oppressive systems stems from a deep motivation to create a more equitable and just world. Social movements, fueled by collective motivation, have reshaped societal norms and institutions.

On a global scale, motivation has driven nations to collaborate and address shared challenges. From scientific endeavors to combating global issues like climate change, the collective motivation of humankind has led to international collaborations and agreements. The aspiration for a better world transcends borders, driven by a shared motivation to address global challenges collectively.

The pursuit of higher standards is intrinsic to human nature. Motivation is the force that compels individuals and societies to seek continuous improvement. Whether in the realms of education, technology, healthcare, or governance, the motivation to surpass existing standards and achieve new heights fosters a culture of progress.

Motivation serves as a beacon of resilience in the face of challenges. Societies motivated to overcome adversity, whether it be through technological innovation in response to crises or collective efforts to rebuild after disasters, showcase the indomitable spirit that motivation instills.

In conclusion, motivation is a dynamic and transformative force that permeates every facet of society. It fuels the pursuit of progress, economic development, cultural richness, social justice, and global collaboration. The collective motivation of humankind has pushed societies to higher and higher standards, shaping the course of history and contributing to the continuous evolution of our shared human experience. Remember that even though things can be difficult and you don't want to do it, Motivation is the key to being a better you.

Chapter 2: Structure and Routine

Structures and Routines are seen and used on a day-to-day basis. You may see it during a job or how schools implement it to set forth what will occur that day for the kids. In society, structure and routine is a very common thing and is extremely helpful when trying to reign in the chaos of the average day. It helps to keep people on their feet and know what's to come next.

Why Structure is Important

Structure is a fundamental element that plays a crucial role in shaping and enriching my life. From daily routines to overarching plans, the presence of structure provides a sense of order and purpose, contributing to both personal well-being and professional growth.

In the realm of daily life, having a structured routine serves as a linchpin for effective Time Management. Establishing set times for waking up, meals, work, and leisure activities helps me make the most of each day. For instance, a morning routine that includes exercise and meditation sets a positive tone for the day, fostering a sense of accomplishment and well-being.

The importance of structure becomes evident in Goal Achievement. Whether it's pursuing educational milestones, career objectives, or personal aspirations, having a structured plan delineates the steps needed for success. For instance, breaking down a large project into smaller, manageable tasks with deadlines creates a roadmap, making the goal more achievable.

Structure acts as a buffer against the stress induced by the unknown. When faced with uncertainties, having predetermined plans in place provides a sense of control. For example, maintaining a structured financial plan or emergency preparedness checklist helps alleviate anxiety about unforeseen circumstances, allowing me to navigate challenges with greater confidence.

Healthy Habits find a conducive environment within a structured lifestyle. Setting specific times for meals, exercise, and self-care ensures that health-related activities are integrated seamlessly into daily life. This might involve meal prepping on Sundays or scheduling regular fitness sessions, making it easier to prioritize well-being.

In the professional sphere, structure is a cornerstone of Efficiency and Productivity. Creating a structured work environment, organizing tasks, and setting priorities contribute to a more effective and streamlined workflow. For instance, using project management tools to outline tasks and deadlines enhances collaboration and ensures projects are completed on time.

Socially, structure fosters meaningful connections. Whether it's planning regular family dinners, setting aside time for friends, or participating in community activities, having a structured approach to social interactions ensures that relationships receive the attention they deserve. This might involve scheduling regular catch-ups or planning activities that strengthen bonds.

The importance of structure extends to personal development. Having a structured plan for continuous learning and skill-building ensures ongoing growth. For example, setting aside time for reading, online courses, or skill development workshops forms a structured approach to staying relevant and evolving in a dynamic world.

Psychologically, the importance of structure in human behavior is profound, influencing cognitive processes, emotional well-being, and overall mental health. Structure reduces the cognitive load on the brain by providing predictability and routine. When tasks and activities follow a familiar pattern, the brain doesn't need to constantly reevaluate and make new decisions, conserving mental energy.

Structure instills a sense of control over one's environment. Predictable routines create a feeling of mastery and empowerment, allowing individuals to navigate their lives with a greater sense of confidence. Structure enhances focus and productivity by minimizing distractions. When individuals operate within a structured framework, they are better able to allocate mental resources to the task at hand.

In summary, the psychological impact of structure on human behavior is extensive. From reducing cognitive load and fostering a sense of control to mitigating stress and shaping habits, structure plays a pivotal role in promoting mental well-being and influencing how individuals navigate the complexities of daily life.

The Effectiveness of Structure

STRUCTURE IS A POWERFUL tool that permeates various aspects of my life, enhancing effectiveness and contributing to overall well-being. Take, for example, the structured morning routine. It creates a seamless start to the day, allowing you to transition from sleep to productivity without the mental burden of decision-making. This routine includes specific times for waking up, exercise, and a nutritious breakfast, setting a positive tone for the day ahead. Having a morning routine will gradually make you feel better and not sleep the day away.

In professional life, the effectiveness of structure is evident in project management. Utilizing structured frameworks and timelines ensures that tasks are organized, priorities are clear, and deadlines are met. This approach enhances efficiency, minimizes the risk of overlooking crucial details, and promotes a smooth workflow. It allows me to navigate complex projects with a clear plan of action, ultimately contributing to successful outcomes. This helps dramatically for jobs with a high workload or many cogs that need to be moved or reviewed. For those who are self-employed, this helps tremendously so that you are being efficient and able to know what you need to do and when to do it.

Financial planning is another area where structure proves invaluable. Implementing a budget, savings plan, and investment strategy creates a structured approach to managing finances. This not only fosters financial stability but also reduces stress associated with money management. The predictability of a well-structured financial plan provides a sense of control and allows for more intentional decision-making. With structure to your finances, you will notice your savings slowly increasing, more spending money available, and less worry regarding whether you will have enough for the next bill or disaster that might occur.

On a personal level, the effectiveness of structure extends to self-care. A structured approach to health and well-being, including regular exercise, balanced nutrition, and sufficient sleep, forms the foundation for a healthy lifestyle. By incorporating these habits into a structured routine, I proactively prioritize my physical and mental well-being, reaping long-term benefits. You will notice having more time to actually go to the gym or out for a nice walk. If you continue your structured routine you will even notice weight loss or muscle gain. You can find time to cook more at home instead of spending money on that fast food or focusing on things you never thought you had the time for and getting it accomplished. I have even implemented structure into my lifestyle so that I could even write this book within a month.

In social interactions, the effectiveness of structure is evident in maintaining relationships. Whether it's scheduling regular catch-ups with friends or planning family gatherings, having a structured approach to social engagements ensures that relationships receive the attention they deserve. This contributes to the cultivation of meaningful connections and strengthens the support system around you.

Guidelines for Creating a Routine

In the realm of daily routines, the key lies in establishing a choreography for each day, a rhythm that orchestrates productivity, self-care, and moments of respite.

Morning

Begin with the sunrise, allowing the morning to unfold as the opening chapter of your day. Designate this time for activities that set a positive tone—perhaps exercise, meditation, or a nutritious breakfast. If you work in the morning, try to wake up atleast an hour before you need to go to work. This single hour makes a huge difference in your morning routine. Many people usually will wake up and head to work in a rush which sets your whole day off in an annoyed mood. Adding that single hour gives you time to face the day while preparing smaller things. That single hour could help your mood for the day go from a negative to a more positive mood.

In the morning always stretch and loosen up your body as it has been laying still for multiple hours. Stretching helps move blood flow allowing your body to get up and running faster than usual.

Mid-Day

As the day progresses, allocate focused time blocks for work or study, interspersed with strategic breaks to rejuvenate the mind. Weave self-care practices into the narrative, such as a midday walk, healthy meals, and moments of mindfulness. For those still working or in school, continue to work and learn, but also find those pockets of time to de-stress and unplug from the day. This can be difficult especially if you are in school or with a job that has to have you constantly working, but try to find just that moment that you can take some time for yourself. If you don't work during this time or it is the weekend, try to be productive during this time. Use this time to work on things that need to be done or things you would like to be done, generally chores, learning, working on side projects, and other things that you would like to get done.

EVENING

As the evening descends, create a gentle wind-down routine, signaling to both body and mind that it's time to transition into a state of restful repose. This is when you would start doing things that are less productive regarding using your brain and more about soothing things. Oddly enough, working out is a great soothing thing a few hours before bedtime. The body gets to work out its excess energy while burning calories that were not used during the day making it easier to sleep instead of insomnia kicking in. Use this time to catch up on things you wish to read or make. With your brain slowing down from productiveness, your mind begins to wonder and allow more creative thoughts to flow through. If you wish to work on a hobby or attend something that is soothing to you, now is the time. It's also recommended to bathe. Showering or soaking in the tub is just like exercising in the sense that it helps the body release the everyday tensions and allows a better sleep.

Night Time

During this time you should be preparing to go to sleep. Try to stay on time with your sleep schedule. For those working the night shift, reverse the order within the daily routine. Try not to be on your phone about an hour before bed. It seems like the most reasonable thing to do as scrolling through your phone due to boredom or something to catch up on as you lay down, but even having the phone on the lowest brightness affects the eyes causing your retina to absorb more light making it harder to sleep leading to insomnia. When you go to be try to find your comfort spot which most people have without knowing. Some people sleep on their backs, sides, stomachs, or a combination of both. When lying in bed, try to let your mind wander. Do not think about the next day and what you need to do as it goes against the purpose of your routine and causes you to overthink, instead think of things that you may enjoy or recall a memory that made you feel good.

Some practices involve having a certain thought that helps you go to sleep. For example. Some people think of a scenery and imagine it in their head going over every detail like staring into the horizon by the ocean or sitting in a cabin watching the snow fall down. If you continue to think of these images when you go to sleep it hardwires your brain to learn it is time to sleep while also helping you relax.

Commitment and Flexibility

Commitment to a daily routine is a dynamic force that breathes life into our intentions, transforming aspirations into tangible reality. This commitment, like the steady heartbeat of a well-orchestrated symphony, infuses purpose into each action, providing the structure necessary to navigate the complexities of daily life with intentionality and resilience. In the tapestry of our daily lives, consistency is woven through the threads of habit formation. A committed routine becomes the loom upon which these habits are crafted, with regular engagement in specific activities at designated times establishing behavioral patterns that become second nature.

Beyond the realm of habit, commitment to a routine emerges as a powerful ally in the pursuit of our goals. This commitment propels us forward, infusing each day with a focused effort that accumulates over time, propelling us steadily toward our objectives.

Central to the concept of commitment to routine is the art of time management. By adhering to a set schedule, we optimize the use of our time, ensuring that tasks and activities are not only completed efficiently but also aligned with our overarching goals and priorities.

Life is, inevitably, filled with unexpected challenges. Here, the committed routine takes on the role of a stabilizing force, providing a framework through which we navigate disruptions and bounce back from setbacks with resilience and adaptability.

In the realm of mental well-being, the commitment to self-care routines becomes a salient contributor. The regular engagement in activities that bring joy, relaxation, and fulfillment becomes a cornerstone of emotional resilience, nurturing a positive and balanced mental state.

Perhaps one of the most significant outcomes of a committed routine is the cultivation of trust in oneself. As we consistently honor our commitments to our daily rhythm, we forge a bond of trust, becoming individuals who reliably follow through on promises made to ourselves. Beyond the short-term intensity and long-term consistency, the committed routine emphasizes the enduring power of sustained effort. The steady progress accrued through a committed approach often surpasses the transient impact of sporadic bursts of intensity.

Finally, commitment to a routine instills a profound sense of control and empowerment. It positions us as active architects of our daily lives, influencing not only how we respond to challenges but also how we shape and define our own narrative.

In conclusion, the commitment to a daily routine transcends the mundane and becomes a potent force for personal development and well-being. It is a disciplined approach to life that transforms intentions into habits, supports goal achievement, and fortifies our resilience. By remaining steadfast in our commitment to routine, we embark on a journey of continuous growth, fulfillment, and intentional living.

In the grand orchestration of our lives, flexibility within our routines emerges as a vital and harmonizing melody. Recognizing the inevitability of unexpected events or opportunities that demand immediate attention, the importance of flexibility lies in its ability to accommodate the unpredictable cadence of life.

Life, by its very nature, is dynamic. Unexpected occurrences, urgent matters, or unforeseen opportunities can disrupt the most meticulously planned routines. It is within this landscape of unpredictability that the true value of flexibility becomes apparent. Rather than rigidly adhering to a predetermined script, a flexible routine allows for improvisation, providing the freedom to adapt to the unforeseen without causing undue stress.

Crucial to the concept of flexibility is the acknowledgment that life is replete with moments that demand our immediate attention. It might be a last-minute work assignment, a family emergency, or an invitation to an impromptu event. A flexible routine allows us to gracefully pivot, ensuring that we can address these pressing matters without feeling confined or overwhelmed by a rigid schedule.

Moreover, carving out free slots within the weekly schedule becomes a strategic maneuver in embracing flexibility. These open spaces serve as blank canvases, ready to accommodate any unexpected occurrences or, conversely, to provide a much-needed breather. Allowing room for spontaneity ensures that the routine remains adaptable, fostering a sense of control amid the unpredictable rhythm of life.

In the spirit of flexibility, the idea of having makeup slots within the schedule becomes an important contingency. These slots act as placeholders, enabling us to catch up on missed tasks or activities when unexpected disruptions occur. They become the safety nets that prevent the routine from unraveling entirely due to the occasional deviation.

HOWEVER, IT'S EQUALLY important to strike a balance between flexibility and accountability. While embracing the unexpected is crucial, allowing too much deviation can lead to a routine losing its intended purpose. This is where a nuanced understanding of flexibility comes into play — the ability to adjust without completely abandoning the structure that keeps our lives organized and productive.

There's wisdom in recognizing that some weeks might not unfold as planned. Life's demands can be relentless, and there will be instances where certain routine elements need to be missed. The key is to approach such deviations with a sense of understanding and self-compassion. Acceptance that missing a week, on occasion, is not a failure but a testament to our ability to adapt and prioritize as needed.

The importance of flexibility in routine lies in its capacity to harmonize the structured and spontaneous elements of our lives. It allows us to navigate the unexpected with grace, ensuring that our routines remain adaptive, resilient, and, above all, aligned with the ebb and flow of life. Embracing flexibility fosters a mindset of balance, enabling us to navigate the unpredictable while maintaining a sense of control and intentionality in our daily lives.

Time Management and Reviewing Your Routine

Time management when it comes to a routine is one of the most important factors when making your routine and keeping it going. A lot of issues with people who make a routine is when they allow too little or too much time for a task to be done. The best way to handle this is to implement a weekly schedule for breathing room and flexibility. If you pile up multiple tasks within a single day, it will feel more like work and make it harder to keep you motivated and sticking to the routine. It also makes it harder with how life may throw curveballs at you. Try to find that niche within your weekly schedule of when to assign things on what days. If you have more free time on a certain day, make it the day to be productive. If you have a day that is just already maxed, make it a day with very few tasks, but never miss a day without having something within a task to do. Even a small thing can help hold the momentum to the next day so that you stay committed to your schedule.

Things can change every day or you find that some things are just physically not possible or a task that you wish to work on no longer makes sense or has been completed and no longer needs to be done. This is a time to review your schedule. Take once a month to review your usual weekly schedule and go over each task and what they are.

Are they still efficient? Should you put them in a different slot? Should you let go of a task or a new one? The idea is to find that perfect rhythm where everything fits perfectly. When everything is running smoothly, it will feel like everything makes sense and there will be no stress or struggle performing the tasks assigned in your schedule. The overall goal of a routine is to better help yourself while improving and completing things you wish could get done. With a proper routine, there isn't anything you can't accomplish. Remember to be flexible, consistent, and diligent so that you do better.

Chapter 3: Money

Money holds a pivotal role in the fabric of an individual's life, weaving through various aspects and influencing the pursuit of well-being. Beyond its tangible form, money serves as a conduit for meeting fundamental needs, acting as the cornerstone for survival. The ability to procure food, secure shelter, and access healthcare hinges on financial resources, establishing a baseline for a dignified existence. The importance of money extends beyond mere survival, permeating into the realms of security and stability. Financial resources offer a buffer against unforeseen circumstances, empowering individuals to navigate the unpredictable terrain of life with confidence.

Whether facing a medical emergency or unexpected expenses, having financial means provides a safety net, mitigating the impact of uncertainties and fostering a sense of resilience. Moreover, money is not solely a tool for immediate survival but a catalyst for long-term planning and aspirations. It serves as a vehicle for individuals to envision and realize their future goals. From pursuing education to investing in personal development, financial resources enable the construction of a path towards self-improvement and advancement. The ability to plan for the future, save for significant milestones, and invest in one's growth contributes to a sense of agency and purpose. Money facilitates access to opportunities that transcend the necessities of life.

Education, a key driver of personal and societal progress, often requires financial investment. From acquiring skills to pursuing higher education, the financial dimension becomes a gateway to knowledge and self-improvement. Similarly, travel and exposure to diverse experiences, which contribute to personal growth, are often contingent on financial means. While acknowledging the significance of money in enhancing the quality of life, it is essential to recognize its limits in dictating happiness. Money can provide comfort and convenience, but true fulfillment emerges from meaningful connections, personal achievements, and a sense of purpose. Striking a balance between financial well-being and holistic life satisfaction is crucial.

How to Save Money

Saving money is a prudent financial practice that empowers individuals to build a secure future, handle unexpected expenses, and achieve long-term goals. Adopting effective saving methods is essential in cultivating a sustainable financial lifestyle. Here are various strategies to help individuals save money.

Create a Budget:

Establishing a budget is the foundational step in any savings plan. Categorize monthly income and allocate specific amounts to essential expenses, discretionary spending, and savings. This provides a clear overview of financial inflows and outflows, making identifying areas for potential savings easier. Make sure that the budget covers all of your bills and expenses. Make sure you also allocate money towards things that can range such as groceries or gas that shift constantly.

Automate Savings:

Setting up automated transfers to a dedicated savings account ensures consistency in saving. By automating the process, a predetermined portion of income is seamlessly directed towards savings, reducing the temptation to spend impulsively. This can help towards things that you wish to save up for with larger purchasing items such as household replacements, vehicles, or even a simple vacation.

Emergency Fund:

Building an emergency fund is crucial for financial resilience. Allocate a portion of savings to create a fund that covers three to six months' worth of living expenses. This fund acts as a financial cushion during unforeseen circumstances, mitigating the need to dip into other savings or accumulate debt. It may seem like money just sitting, but life can be very dynamic which causes turmoil from losing a job, a loved one, or a disaster, With that emergency fund, it can truly be a critical thing that helps under the most stressful situations. Try your hardest to only use this money for very serious things you may need.

Cut Unnecessary Expenses:

Conduct a thorough analysis of spending habits to identify areas where costs can be trimmed. This may involve canceling unused subscriptions, cooking at home instead of dining out, or opting for cost-effective alternatives without compromising on quality. You would be surprised what we spend a month on things when we look at our budgets. Cooking at home instead of ordering out is a huge price difference when it comes to money. Some people may have a bad habit of spending money online shopping for things they want, but don't necessarily have. Try to limit your purchase of things by setting limits per month to help save you money that can go towards something more important.

Negotiate Bills:

Regularly review utility bills, insurance premiums, and subscription costs. Negotiating with service providers or exploring competitive options can lead to reduced monthly expenses, contributing to overall savings. A lot of people feel comfortable about staying with the same provider because it seems more of a hassle to switch. In some cases, this can be true, but sometimes you can save more money by bundling bills under a new provider or even working with a new bank with better returns and benefits.

Shop Smart:

Practice mindful spending by comparing prices, utilizing discounts, and taking advantage of cashback or rewards programs. Prioritize needs over wants and consider buying generic or store-brand products to save on everyday expenses. Coupons and sales opportunities occur often across all stores, use these to your advantage to get more bang for your buck. Some generic brands are cheaper, but are essentially the same product and done so as a way for the markets to compete against other brands.

How to Spend Money

Effective money management involves a holistic approach that extends beyond saving, encompassing the strategic allocation of resources to achieve both immediate needs and future financial objectives. Defining clear financial goals provides a crucial foundation, guiding spending decisions toward outcomes that align with one's aspirations. Prioritizing needs over wants is a fundamental principle, ensuring that essential expenses take precedence in budget allocations, thereby establishing a robust financial base. Implementing a budget isn't solely about saving; it serves as a practical tool for efficient spending. By allocating specific amounts to different spending categories, individuals create a structured framework that helps prevent unnecessary expenses and fosters disciplined financial habits. Researching and comparing prices before making purchases is a valuable practice, leveraging online resources and tools to maximize the value derived from each expenditure.

Leveraging technology and rewards programs can be advantageous in the pursuit of efficient spending. Utilizing apps to track spending habits allows for a nuanced understanding of financial patterns, while rewards programs from credit cards or retailers offer opportunities for cashback, discounts, or loyalty points, enhancing overall value. Emphasizing quality over quantity is a guiding principle, encouraging individuals to invest in durable, high-quality products that, despite potentially higher upfront costs, often yield long-term savings by minimizing the need for frequent replacements. Investing in education, certifications, or skill development constitutes spending with a future return. Such investments enhance professional capabilities, expanding opportunities for higher income down the road. Housing choices also play a role in long-term financial planning, with individuals encouraged to consider properties that align with their needs without unnecessary extravagance.

Health and wellness expenditures, while involving spending, contribute significantly to long-term well-being, potentially reducing future medical costs. Regularly evaluating subscription services and discontinuing unused or unnecessary subscriptions is a practical approach to prevent funds from trickling away unnoticed. Avoiding impulse spending by implementing a cooling-off period for significant purchases fosters thoughtful consideration, reducing the likelihood of regrettable or unnecessary expenses. Tax-efficient spending strategies, such as contributing to retirement accounts or eligible education expenses, can optimize overall financial outcomes.

Opting for budget-friendly grocery shopping instead of dining out is a practical choice that not only helps manage expenses but also provides control over food choices and fosters essential cooking skills. A weekly meal plan is a cornerstone in this approach, allowing you to outline the meals you intend to prepare and identify ingredients that can be used across multiple dishes. This not only minimizes waste but also streamlines your shopping list, preventing impulse purchases. Crafting a detailed shopping list based on your meal plan is key. It helps you stay focused on essential items and reduces the likelihood of spontaneous purchases that can contribute to overspending.

Consider purchasing non-perishable items in bulk as they often come at a lower unit cost. Staples like rice, pasta, canned goods, and grains can be bought in larger quantities, contributing to long-term savings. Prioritize seasonal and locally sourced produce for both cost savings and enhanced flavor. Generic or store brands are viable alternatives to name brands, offering cost savings without compromising quality. Keep an eye out for coupons, discounts, and loyalty programs offered by grocery stores to further reduce your overall bill. Be strategic in your shopping approach. Take advantage of sales and promotions, and consider shopping during off-peak hours to avoid impulse purchases. When perishable items are on sale, purchase in larger quantities and freeze what you won't use immediately to prevent spoilage and take advantage of bulk discounts.

Opt for preparing convenience foods at home instead of buying pre-packaged and processed options. This not only saves money but also allows you to control the ingredients, contributing to healthier meals. Limit the purchase of pre-packaged snacks and opt for cost-effective alternatives like fresh fruits, nuts, or homemade snacks to save on your grocery bill. Compare unit prices to identify the most cost-effective options, considering package sizes and potential waste. Embrace leftovers as a budget-friendly strategy by cooking larger portions and planning meals that can be repurposed the next day. By adopting these budget-friendly grocery shopping practices, individuals can transform their culinary habits, save money, and enjoy the added benefits of healthier and more personalized meals prepared in the comfort of their kitchens.

How to Earn Money

In the contemporary landscape of work and finance, the avenues for earning money have expanded beyond the traditional realms of employment. Diversifying income streams is a strategic approach that not only provides financial stability but also opens up opportunities for personal and professional growth. Traditional employment remains a foundational source of income for many individuals. Working for a company or organization in a full-time or part-time capacity provides a stable and consistent paycheck. Exploring different job opportunities within one's field or considering career advancement can contribute to increased earnings. At the end of the day, a job is the best way to earn your money with many different varieties that vary from experience and work.

The rise of gig or side jobs has paved the way for freelancing and online job opportunities. Platforms like Upwork, Freelancer, and Fiverr connect freelancers with clients seeking services ranging from writing and graphic design to programming and digital marketing. Remote work options have expanded, offering a diverse array of roles that cater to various skill sets. You can also now do many jobs online right from your home. All you would need is a stable internet connection, a computer, and a few other office equipment depending on the job.

For those with entrepreneurial ambitions, starting a side business or an online venture can be a rewarding endeavor. E-commerce platforms provide an avenue for selling products, whether they are handmade crafts, vintage items, artwork, or unique creations. Turning a passion or hobby into a business can not only generate income but also bring a sense of fulfillment.

Building wealth through passive income investments involves putting money into assets that generate returns with minimal effort. This can include dividend-paying stocks, real estate investments, peer-to-peer lending, and creating an investment portfolio. The goal is to create streams of income that require less active involvement over time.

With social media becoming a huge source of entertainment for everyone as well as news, content creators can explore opportunities in affiliate marketing and blogging. Affiliate marketing involves promoting products and earning a commission for each sale made through one's referral. Blogging, whether through sponsored content or ad revenue, can become a source of income as the audience grows.

The ideal goal is to earn money that fits your needs while also providing a cushion for the future. Make sure not to overexert yourself for money as burnout can lead to hating your passion projects and your job. Use your various skills and talents to make money in a way only you can do. Whether it's through beautiful artwork or special food you may make, using your skills to earn money will assist you greatly.

The End Goal of Your Income

THE PURSUIT OF EARNING money is not merely a means to an end; rather, it's a strategic journey toward achieving long-term financial well-being and securing a comfortable and fulfilling life. As individuals accumulate wealth, the focus often shifts towards making impactful long-term purchases and investments that contribute to a secure and enjoyable future. One of the significant long-term purchases that many individuals aspire to is homeownership. Investing in a property not only provides a sense of stability but can also serve as a valuable asset that may be appreciated over time. Homeownership not only offers the comfort of a place to call one's own but can also be a strategic financial move.

Investing in education and skill development is a timeless pursuit that pays dividends throughout one's life. Long-term investments in acquiring new skills, and certifications, or even pursuing advanced degrees can enhance career prospects, increase earning potential, and contribute to a more fulfilling professional journey.

For those inclined towards entrepreneurship, investing in and building successful ventures can be a long-term pursuit. Starting and growing a business not only has the potential for financial returns but also offers a sense of accomplishment and the opportunity to leave a lasting legacy. While financial planning often focuses on tangible assets, long-term purchases can also include investments in experiences. Travel, cultural exploration, and engaging in enriching activities contribute to a fulfilling life. These experiences, while intangible, can create lasting memories and enrich one's perspective.

AS INDIVIDUALS ACCUMULATE wealth, the desire to make a positive impact on society often becomes a significant motivator. Long-term investments in philanthropy and giving back to the community can create a legacy of social responsibility and contribute to the betterment of the world.

In conclusion, the end goal of earning money extends far beyond immediate needs and desires. It involves thoughtful consideration of long-term purchases and investments that contribute to financial security, personal growth, and a meaningful and enjoyable life. Balancing immediate gratification with prudent planning for the future is the essence of a well-rounded approach to wealth management and will make you better at your core.

Chapter 4: Physical Attributes

―――

The human body is a marvel of intricate design, comprising numerous physical attributes that work synergistically to sustain life and enable a wide range of activities. From the microscopic level of cells to the complex systems that govern our movement and perception, the human body operates with remarkable precision.

At the cellular level, the human body is composed of trillions of cells, each with specific functions and roles. Cells are the basic building blocks of life, and they collaborate to form tissues, organs, and ultimately, organ systems. These organ systems work together to maintain homeostasis, the body's internal balance. The cardiovascular system, for instance, consists of the heart, blood vessels, and blood, working in unison to circulate oxygen, nutrients, and hormones throughout the body and remove waste products.

One of the most apparent physical attributes of the human body is its skeletal structure. The skeletal system provides structural support, protects vital organs, and facilitates movement. Bones, joints, and cartilage collaborate to create a flexible yet sturdy framework. Muscles, attached to bones by tendons, contract and relax to move. This intricate interplay of bones and muscles allows for a wide range of motions, from the subtle flexing of fingers to the powerful strides of walking or running.

The nervous system plays a pivotal role in coordinating and controlling bodily functions. Comprising the central nervous system (CNS) and the peripheral nervous system (PNS), this intricate network of nerves and cells enables communication between different parts of the body. The brain, a highly complex organ, serves as the command center, interpreting sensory information, processing thoughts, and initiating responses. The spinal cord, an extension of the brain, facilitates the transmission of signals between the brain and the rest of the body.

The sensory organs contribute significantly to our perception of the world. The eyes, ears, nose, tongue, and skin work in concert to gather information from the environment. Eyes capture light and convert it into visual signals, while ears detect sound waves and translate them into auditory perceptions. The skin, the body's largest organ, senses touch, pressure, temperature, and pain. These sensory inputs provide crucial information for survival and enhance the overall human experience.

Another essential physical attribute is the respiratory system, responsible for the exchange of gases between the body and the environment. The lungs, in conjunction with the respiratory muscles and airways, facilitate the intake of oxygen and the removal of carbon dioxide. This process, known as respiration, is vital for energy production and maintaining the body's acid-base balance.

The digestive system is paramount for nutrient absorption and energy production. When food enters the mouth, a series of processes unfold as it travels through the esophagus, stomach, and intestines. Enzymes and digestive juices break down complex nutrients into smaller molecules that the body can absorb and utilize. The liver and pancreas play crucial roles in producing digestive enzymes and regulating blood sugar levels.

The endocrine system, comprising glands such as the pituitary, thyroid, and adrenal glands, secretes hormones that regulate various bodily functions. These chemical messengers influence growth, metabolism, reproduction, and stress responses. The endocrine system works with the nervous system to maintain equilibrium within the body.

The immune system, a complex network of cells and proteins, defends the body against harmful invaders such as bacteria, viruses, and toxins. White blood cells, antibodies, and other components collaborate to identify and neutralize foreign substances, providing a crucial defense against infections and diseases.

You may be asking yourself "Why is the anatomy of the human body helpful in becoming a better you?". The answer is simple. To be a better you, you must make sure that at your core, everything is working at the utmost factor. You have to know how your body works to improve it or you will struggle to make any progress with it.

<u>What do You want from Your body?</u>

IN THE PURSUIT OF PHYSICAL well-being, humans often yearn for various transformations to enhance their appearance and overall health. From achieving radiant skin to perfecting posture, losing or gaining weight, and cultivating lustrous hair, the desire for positive changes is a driving force in the lives of many.

The quest for flawless skin is a common aspiration. Humans seek solutions to address concerns such as acne, blemishes, and signs of aging. Skincare routines, comprising cleansers, moisturizers, and serums, have become rituals in the pursuit of a clearer complexion. Additionally, individuals explore dermatological treatments and cosmetic procedures, from chemical peels to laser therapy, as they strive to attain the elusive goal of flawless and youthful skin. Regarding acne and blemishes such as scabs. It is difficult sometimes not to pester them when they either hurt or itch. Try to resist though as creating an open wound on your face allows more bacteria to come into the skin and delays the healing process longer.

Posture plays a crucial role in the way the body carries itself, impacting not only physical health but also confidence and self-perception. Many individuals are drawn to the idea of achieving better posture to alleviate back pain, enhance body language, and project a more confident image. Ergonomic furniture, posture-correcting exercises, and mindfulness practices are among the strategies employed to counteract the effects of sedentary lifestyles and promote optimal alignment. The next time you are having a conversation with an individual or events throughout the day, take the time to think about your posture and how it is. You may find yourself slouching without even noticing it. To combat this, try and stretch your back straight up every hour to get your body used to better posture. Another thing to help is stretching early in the morning which not only helps you wake up, but releases the stiffness of your muscles.

Weight management is a perennial concern for individuals with diverse goals. While some embark on weight loss journeys to improve health or boost self-esteem, others strive to gain weight for various reasons, including athletic performance or overcoming undernutrition. Diets, exercise regimens, and, in some cases, medical interventions are sought to achieve and maintain the desired weight. The cultural emphasis on body image has led to an array of approaches, from trendy diets to holistic lifestyle changes, reflecting the multifaceted nature of this pursuit. We will discuss both weight loss and gaining muscle later in this chapter.

The desire to have healthy, vibrant hair is deeply ingrained in human culture and personal identity. Individuals often seek remedies for issues such as hair loss, dullness, or brittleness. Haircare routines involve an array of products, including shampoos, conditioners, and styling aids. Furthermore, the pursuit of optimal hair health extends to dietary choices, with an emphasis on nutrients like vitamins and proteins believed to contribute to lustrous locks. Some may explore hair treatments, ranging from salon procedures to home remedies, to address specific concerns and achieve their ideal mane. Sadly, genetics play a large role in hair in both growing too much or having too little. You can continue to try new treatments as more and more come out every year or you can change your perspective and accept the way you are learning things to assist with lack of hair or having too much.

Losing weight is a prevalent goal for many, driven by health considerations, societal standards, or personal aspirations. The weight loss journey often involves a combination of dietary modifications, regular exercise, and lifestyle changes. Fad diets and fitness trends ebb and flow, with individuals experimenting with various approaches to find what works best for them. The motivations behind weight loss are diverse, encompassing improved physical health, increased energy levels, and a desire to fit societal beauty standards.

On the flip side, gaining weight can be a goal for those looking to build muscle, recover from illness, or address concerns related to underweight conditions. Individuals seeking weight gain may adopt strength training routines, increase calorie intake, and explore nutritional supplements to achieve their objectives. This pursuit is often accompanied by a focus on overall health, ensuring that the weight gained consists of muscle rather than unhealthy fat. We will discuss this later in the chapter on some things you can do to make your diet.

In the intricate tapestry of human desires for physical transformation, the common thread is the pursuit of well-being and self-improvement. The diverse approaches individuals take to achieve their goals reflect the complexity of human motivations and the evolving nature of societal ideals.

One thing that needs to be addressed though is that changing and improving your body can better yourself, but there are things no matter how we try can not be changed either due to health, genetics, or technology not advanced enough for these changes. We have to learn to accept what makes us unique and not hate or despise what makes us so. To be bald or to have an appendage missing does not make you less of a human being. We are all humans who have a story and genetic makeup that is different from each person. Don't ever be ashamed of who you are as that is not what this chapter is about. This chapter is to assist you in improving yourself so that can be worked on and graspable.

Regiment of Physical Activity

A BODY IN MOTION IN motion stays in motion as they say. Embarking on a well-rounded and effective physical activity regimen is a cornerstone of promoting overall health and fitness. Such regimens often incorporate a variety of workout routines, outdoor activities, and calorie-burning exercises to cater to different aspects of physical well-being. A comprehensive fitness routine encompasses both cardiovascular exercises and strength training, providing a holistic approach to building endurance, strength, and flexibility.

Cardiovascular exercises form a crucial component of any physical activity regimen, contributing to heart health, weight management, and overall vitality. Engaging in activities such as running, cycling, or swimming helps elevate the heart rate and improve cardiovascular endurance. These exercises not only burn calories but also enhance lung capacity, promoting efficient oxygen circulation throughout the body. Incorporating a mix of high-intensity interval training (HIIT) and steady-state cardio sessions adds diversity to the routine, keeping the body challenged and preventing monotony. The more you incorporate HIIT the easier it gets also. This exercise seems to be the harder one for people to follow as your body and mind are set to conserve energy, but we have to get past this and rewrite our minds to yearn for it instead of finding excuses not to do it.

In addition to structured workout routines, integrating walks into the daily routine offers a simple yet effective way to boost physical activity. Walking is a low-impact exercise accessible to individuals of all fitness levels and ages. It serves as an excellent option for those seeking to burn calories, improve cardiovascular health, and maintain joint mobility. Whether it's a brisk morning walk, an afternoon stroll, or a post-dinner saunter, incorporating regular walks into the routine contributes to overall well-being and aids in weight management. Taking a walk also helps your mind mentally. It is a way to think things over and observe everything around you. Taking a walk can be very soothing and a natural way in a more physical meditation-like state to feel more at peace and to relieve stress.

SPORTS AND RECREATIONAL activities provide an engaging avenue for burning calories while enjoying the social and competitive aspects of physical activity. Participating in team sports like soccer, basketball, or volleyball not only enhances cardiovascular fitness but also promotes teamwork and camaraderie. Additionally, sports such as tennis, swimming, or cycling offer diverse options for those seeking an alternative to traditional workouts. Rock climbing, in particular, combines strength, endurance, and mental focus, providing a full-body workout that challenges both physical and cognitive capabilities. Do not be discouraged if you feel that you have no one to do a sport with. Reach out to other fellow individuals wishing to strive for the same thing. Many groups meet every week to do casual games or those with more competitive play.

Strength training is an integral component of a well-rounded physical activity regimen, contributing to muscle development, bone density, and metabolic health. Incorporating resistance training exercises, whether using free weights, resistance bands, or bodyweight exercises, helps build lean muscle mass and boosts the body's calorie-burning capacity. Targeting major muscle groups with exercises like squats, deadlifts, and bench presses ensures a balanced approach to strength training. Try and do some research before you head to the gym to lift weights as a smarter mind can execute the exercises correctly and guide you to a more synergistic routine for key muscle groups. Having a friend with you also helps you stay on track with your routine when it comes to going to the gym.

Flexibility and mobility exercises are often overlooked but are crucial for maintaining joint health and preventing injuries. Activities such as yoga or Pilates improve flexibility, balance, and core strength. These practices not only contribute to physical fitness but also foster mindfulness and stress reduction, addressing the holistic well-being of the individual. Just like stretching in the morning prepares you for the day, flexibility exercises maintain your body through all exercises and help reduce stress, pain, and keeping you going throughout the week.

Remember for all exercises to start off slow, but make sure to be consistent. If you go too hard on your first day, it could make you feel negative subconsciously making it harder to continue said exercise. Always try to maintain consistency so that it becomes accustomed to your routine to do the exercises instead of a chance of not attending or even dropping the exercise altogether.

Diet

Crafting a personalized and effective diet is a nuanced process that requires consideration of individual preferences, lifestyle, and nutritional needs. Rather than adopting a one-size-fits-all approach, creating a diet that works involves understanding the fundamentals of nutrition, the role of calories, and the significance of each food group in supporting overall health.

At the core of any diet is the concept of caloric intake, a fundamental aspect of weight management and overall well-being. Calories represent the energy derived from food, and understanding how many calories the body needs is essential for maintaining a healthy weight. Factors such as age, gender, activity level, and metabolism influence daily caloric requirements. Establishing a balance between caloric intake and expenditure is key to weight maintenance, loss, or gain.

To count calories effectively, one can utilize various tools and resources, including food labels, online databases, or mobile apps. Tracking caloric intake provides insight into dietary patterns and helps individuals make informed choices. However, it's crucial to recognize that not all calories are created equal. Nutrient-dense foods, rich in vitamins, minerals, and other essential nutrients, should be prioritized over empty-calorie options to support overall health.

Understanding the role of each food group is integral to creating a balanced and nutritious diet. The macronutrients—carbohydrates, proteins, and fats—form the foundation of dietary choices. Carbohydrates serve as the body's primary source of energy, and incorporating complex carbohydrates from whole grains, fruits, and vegetables ensures sustained energy levels. Proteins are essential for muscle repair and maintenance, and sources such as lean meats, fish, legumes, and dairy products should be included. Healthy fats, derived from sources like avocados, nuts, and olive oil, play a crucial role in supporting brain function and nutrient absorption.

In addition to macronutrients, micronutrients—vitamins and minerals—play vital roles in various physiological functions. Fruits and vegetables are rich sources of vitamins and minerals, contributing to immune function, bone health, and overall vitality. Balancing different colors and types of fruits and vegetables ensures a diverse array of nutrients.

DAIRY OR DAIRY ALTERNATIVES provide essential calcium for bone health, while lean meats and plant-based proteins supply iron, zinc, and other vital minerals. Whole grains contribute fiber, supporting digestive health and providing a feeling of satiety. Ensuring variety within each food group helps cover a spectrum of nutrients, fostering a well-rounded and nourishing diet.

An example of a meal that exemplifies a balanced diet includes grilled chicken (protein), quinoa (complex carbohydrates), and a colorful array of vegetables (vitamins and minerals). Incorporating olive oil as a dressing adds healthy fats. This meal provides a combination of macronutrients and micronutrients, promoting satiety, energy, and overall nutritional well-being.

Foods to Avoid

In the intricate landscape of dietary choices, certain foods should be approached with caution due to their potential negative impact on health when consumed in excess. It is essential to be mindful of the quality and quantity of the foods we incorporate into our diets, as an imbalanced intake of certain items can contribute to various health concerns. Let's explore some of these foods and the reasons why they should be consumed in moderation.

Highly processed foods laden with added sugars, unhealthy fats, and refined carbohydrates are often culprits in the realm of dietary caution. These products, ranging from sugary snacks to ultra-processed convenience meals, can contribute to weight gain, insulin resistance, and an increased risk of chronic diseases such as type 2 diabetes and cardiovascular issues. The excessive consumption of added sugars, in particular, has been linked to obesity and metabolic disturbances, emphasizing the importance of scrutinizing food labels for hidden sugars.

Trans fats, once seen in many processed and fried foods, have rightfully earned their reputation as one of the most harmful dietary components. These fats, formed through an industrial process that adds hydrogen to liquid vegetable oils, increase the shelf life of products but wreak havoc on cardiovascular health. Trans fats not only raise bad cholesterol (LDL) but also lower good cholesterol (HDL), contributing to an elevated risk of heart disease. vigilant label reading remains crucial to avoid potential exposure.

Excessive salt intake, often derived from processed foods and restaurant meals, is another dietary concern. While sodium is an essential nutrient for bodily functions, surpassing recommended daily limits can lead to high blood pressure, fluid retention, and an increased risk of heart disease. Cutting back on processed and pre-packaged foods and opting for fresh, whole ingredients can significantly contribute to lowering sodium intake and promoting cardiovascular health.

Red and processed meats have been scrutinized for their potential association with various health issues, including colorectal cancer and cardiovascular disease. Processed meats, such as bacon and sausages, often contain additives and preservatives that may contribute to health concerns. While lean, unprocessed meats can be part of a balanced diet, it is advisable to moderate their consumption and explore alternative protein sources, such as legumes, nuts, and plant-based proteins. This can be difficult as most of the population consumes meat on a day to day life. Humans are omnivores though and can eat both meat and plants to gain nutrients so try to slowly add alternative proteins to your food to help cut back on your usual meat intake and it can help considerably.

Sugary beverages, including sodas, energy drinks, and sugary fruit juices, are notorious for their high sugar content and low nutritional value. Regular consumption of these beverages has been linked to weight gain, increased risk of type 2 diabetes, and dental problems. Opting for water, herbal teas, or infused water with natural flavors provides a healthier and hydrating alternative, reducing the intake of empty calories and excessive sugars. This is a struggle for most regarding modern life as soda is a very well-known drink to have. The reason it also feels so addicting and hard to cut out is because of caffeine which is used to give it a little kick, but also a way of triggering a need of usage just like nicotine. Treat soda as you would a cigarette. Try to reduce your intake slowly and then switch to alternatives until the need to drink soda has been eliminated from use. Those who don't drink soda anymore and attempt again notice how strong the taste of the soda is and how upsetting their stomach feels which can be a real eye-opener.

Certain refined carbohydrates, such as white bread, white rice, and sugary cereals, are quickly digested, leading to spikes in blood sugar levels. Prolonged consumption of such high-glycemic-index foods may contribute to insulin resistance and an increased risk of type 2 diabetes. Choosing whole grains, such as brown rice, quinoa, and whole-grain bread, provides a more balanced source of carbohydrates with additional fiber and nutrients.

Remember when creating your diet that you also show consistency and meal prepping by buying the right groceries to make your meals and reducing eating out. You will notice a difference over time not only to your figure, but to your wallet on how much you save.

Viewing your Growth and Proud of your Victories

DOCUMENTING ONE'S EXERCISE and diet routine is a powerful tool that not only provides a roadmap of progress but also serves as a source of motivation. Each loss in weight or the ability to lift heavier weights represents a small victory, a tangible sign of dedication and improvement on the path toward achieving personal fitness goals.

Keeping a journal that meticulously details both dietary choices and exercise routines creates a comprehensive record of the fitness journey. The act of documenting daily meals, snacks, and hydration habits provides valuable insights into nutritional patterns. It allows individuals to track their macronutrient intake, identify areas for improvement, and make informed adjustments to ensure a well-balanced diet. This self-awareness is crucial in establishing sustainable eating habits that align with personal health and fitness objectives.

Similarly, recording exercise routines in a journal provides a clear picture of physical activity levels and progress over time. Whether it's tracking the duration of cardio sessions, the number of sets and reps in strength training, or the intensity of workouts, a journal serves as a tangible representation of effort and consistency. Celebrating achievements, such as running an extra mile or lifting heavier weights, reinforces the positive momentum and motivates individuals to push their boundaries further.

The concept of small victories plays a pivotal role in fostering a positive mindset throughout the fitness journey. Weight loss, for instance, is seldom an overnight transformation but rather a series of incremental successes. Whether it's shedding a few pounds or losing inches, each accomplishment contributes to the overall goal and serves as a testament to perseverance. Similarly, in strength training, the ability to lift progressively heavier weights signifies not only physical strength but also the dedication to continuous improvement.

The journal becomes a dynamic tool for reflection, allowing individuals to analyze what works best for their bodies and what adjustments may be necessary. It provides an opportunity to identify patterns of success and areas that require attention. This self-awareness empowers individuals to make informed decisions about their exercise routines and dietary choices, creating a personalized and sustainable approach to health and fitness.

Moreover, the act of documenting the journey in a tangible form creates a sense of accountability. A journal becomes a contract with oneself, a commitment to the goals outlined within its pages. The process of writing down intentions, progress, setbacks, and reflections establishes a level of mindfulness that transcends the mere physical aspects of exercise and diet. It fosters a deeper connection to the journey and a greater understanding of the holistic nature of health and wellness.

Documenting exercise and diet routines through the use of a journal is a powerful strategy for achieving and maintaining health and fitness goals. The small victories represented by weight loss or increased strength serve as stepping stones toward broader objectives. The journal not only acts as a roadmap, providing a clear trajectory of progress, but also as a source of motivation, accountability, and self-reflection. As individuals continue to move forward on their fitness journey, the journal becomes a living document, capturing the evolving narrative of dedication, improvement, and success. With you following your exercise and diet, it will improve you both physically and mentally you better as an individual.

Chapter 5: Mental Process

Humans stand apart from other animals due to their advanced cognitive abilities and the depth and complexity of their emotions. While many animals exhibit intelligence and basic emotional responses, the human mind is distinguished by its capacity for abstract thought, self-awareness, and the ability to contemplate the past and future. Humans possess a remarkable range of emotions, from profound joy to profound sorrow, and they can express these feelings through language, art, and various forms of communication. The intricacies of human emotions contribute to developing intricate social structures, complex relationships, and the pursuit of meaning and purpose in life. This unique combination of cognitive prowess and emotional depth sets humans apart, allowing them to create cultures, societies, and connections that transcend the capabilities of other species.

But with all this, why does this matter in improving ourselves? Humankind unlike other creatures doesn't always go off instinct or survival. We make very odd decisions based on our psyche which contributes to every decision we have made since we gained consciousness. Sometimes our emotions run hot and unable to keep control while other emotions cause of to either care less or make appropriate decisions which affects us greatly. The key to all of this is to look inward and understand our emotions so that we can have control over them and have control over our lives.

Your Identity

The human psyche is an intricate tapestry woven from various components that collectively contribute to the formation of unique personalities. These components encompass cognitive, emotional, and social aspects, all of which are profoundly influenced by the environment in which an individual is raised and the observations they make throughout their lives.

At the core of the human psyche lies cognition, the mental processes that involve acquiring, processing, and utilizing information. Cognitive development begins in early childhood and continues throughout life, shaping one's perception of the world. Children absorb knowledge from their surroundings, learning language, social norms, and problem-solving skills by observing and interacting with caregivers, peers, and the environment. This cognitive foundation becomes the lens through which individuals interpret experiences, leading to diverse thought patterns and intellectual capabilities. Try to observe a parent and a child. The child constantly learns mannerisms and how to act regarding a parent. The child may even pick up habits or try to imitate a parent's actions.

Emotions are another integral facet of the human psyche, adding richness and depth to individual personalities. Emotional development begins in infancy, with caregivers playing a crucial role in the early formation of emotional bonds and regulation. The ability to understand, express, and manage emotions is honed through experiences and interactions. Children raised in nurturing environments may develop secure attachments, fostering emotional resilience and empathy. Conversely, adverse experiences may contribute to the development of maladaptive emotional responses, potentially leading to challenges in interpersonal relationships and mental well-being. Now this isn't always the case as a child from a broken home can have more positive attributes than a child coming from a loving home, but there is a higher chance the child will have positive attributes with a loving and caring home.

Socialization further shapes the human psyche, as individuals navigate the complexities of interpersonal dynamics within family, peer groups, and broader societal contexts. Social norms, cultural values, and familial expectations significantly influence behavior and identity formation. Observing and internalizing social cues, individuals construct a sense of self and develop interpersonal skills that guide interactions with others. This social dimension of the psyche contributes to the diversity of personalities, as cultural and environmental influences shape beliefs, attitudes, and communication styles. This can be seen in the early teens when teenagers start to express themselves more and try to find themselves and the group they belong. Everyone can look back and notice that there were cliques or groups within a school for each and every group. As they say "Birds of a feather stick together".

The impact of upbringing and observation on the human psyche extends beyond childhood, influencing personality traits and behavioral tendencies throughout adulthood. The nature versus nurture debate underscores the interplay between genetic predispositions and environmental factors in shaping individual differences. While genetics contribute to the baseline characteristics of an individual, the environment acts as a mold, shaping and refining these inherent traits. Observational learning continues to play a pivotal role, with adults assimilating new information and adapting their behaviors based on the experiences and examples they encounter.

With all of this information, it is time to identify yourself. Look deep within yourself and hold that mirror up. Who are you? What are your characteristics? What do you love and hate? And with each question ask yourself why. It is easy to know what you are or identify what you love or hate, but it is much harder to identify why you enjoy or hate it. The reason for identifying ourselves internally is so that we can see what people might think of us or what we think of ourselves and what needs to be worked on. The more knowledge of who you are the more control you can have over yourself.

<u>Fears</u>

Fear is a primal and universal emotion deeply ingrained in the human experience. Defined as an emotional response to a perceived threat or danger, fear serves a fundamental purpose in ensuring survival. The roots of fear can be traced back to our evolutionary history, where early humans faced numerous life-threatening situations. The ability to experience fear and respond appropriately to potential dangers provided an evolutionary advantage, allowing individuals to avoid harm and increase their chances of survival.

The physiological and psychological components of fear are interconnected, creating a complex response that prepares the body for a "fight or flight" reaction. When faced with a perceived threat, the amygdala, a key brain structure, triggers the release of stress hormones like adrenaline, preparing the body to confront or escape the danger. Simultaneously, cognitive processes heighten awareness, sharpening focus on the threat at hand. These intricate mechanisms highlight fear's adaptive nature, a mechanism finely tuned over generations to enhance human survival.

Common fears often stem from a combination of instinctual responses and childhood experiences. Fear of heights (acrophobia), for example, can be linked to an evolutionary instinct to avoid precarious situations that could lead to injury or death. Similarly, the fear of snakes or spiders (ophidiophobia and arachnophobia) may be rooted in ancestral environments where encounters with venomous creatures pose genuine threats. These instinctual fears are not inherent at birth but are thought to develop as a result of the evolutionary advantage conferred to those who learned to avoid potential dangers.

Childhood development plays a crucial role in shaping individual fears. Early experiences, especially those involving trauma or distress, can imprint lasting impressions on the developing psyche. For instance, a child who experiences a traumatic event, such as a dog bite, may develop a fear of dogs (cynophobia) later in life. The impact of childhood experiences on fear extends beyond specific incidents, encompassing the broader environment and the quality of caregiving. A secure and nurturing childhood tends to foster a sense of safety, while adverse experiences may contribute to heightened anxiety and a predisposition to fear.

Social learning also contributes to the acquisition of fears during childhood. Children often observe and learn from the reactions of caregivers and peers. If a parent displays fear or anxiety towards certain situations or objects, children are more likely to adopt similar responses through a process known as vicarious learning. This social aspect of fear acquisition underscores the importance of early environments in shaping not only individual fears but also collective fears within a cultural context.

While fear remains an integral part of the human experience, its manifestation and intensity vary widely among individuals. Some fears are universal, rooted in evolutionary history, while others are deeply personal, and shaped by unique life experiences. Understanding the nature of fear and its origins provides valuable insights into the intricacies of human psychology. It allows us to appreciate the adaptive function of fear in promoting survival, while also recognizing the complex interplay of genetics, environment, and personal history that contribute to the diverse array of fears observed in the human population.

Now that you know what fear is for humans, what is it that you are fearful of and how does it affect your daily life? Just like holding up the mirror before, do it again and deep into your psyche to go over some things that may be locked up tight. Your mind tries its hardest to keep those traumatic events away as it is harmful to the person, but sometimes we have to re-visit them and go over the trauma regarding the issue itself.

Your Mental Health

Over the past decade, there has been a transformative shift in societal attitudes towards mental health, marked by increased awareness and a growing recognition of its profound importance. The stigmatization surrounding mental health issues has significantly diminished, and a collective effort has emerged to prioritize mental well-being as an integral component of overall health. This shift is reflective of a broader understanding that mental health is not merely the absence of illness but a dynamic state that influences every aspect of our lives.

Various types of mental health concerns, such as stress, anxiety, and depression, have come to the forefront of public discourse. Stress, often considered a natural response to challenging situations, has been reevaluated in the context of its prolonged and chronic effects on mental health. Awareness campaigns and educational initiatives have highlighted the impact of chronic stress on physical health, emphasizing the need for effective stress management strategies to prevent long-term consequences. There is no human being on this earth who has not felt stress. Everyone has had stress and sadly some more than others. The key is to mitigate it and help stop prolonged stress as it could end in burnout. This can be seen in jobs specifically with high levels of stress. The more you are stressed without relief the more likely you are to get burnout and a hatred for what it is you are doing.

Anxiety, a prevalent mental health condition, has garnered increased attention in the past decade. With more individuals openly sharing their experiences, the public has gained a deeper understanding of the diverse manifestations of anxiety disorders. The recognition that anxiety can significantly affect day-to-day functioning has prompted a shift towards proactive measures, including therapy, mindfulness practices, and lifestyle changes, to manage and mitigate its impact. Anxiety is another well-known factor in society. Anxiety stems from fear itself and can even become physical resulting in a panic attack which has an intense feeling of doom. Your breath could become shallow and quicker while you begin to feel clammy. Panic attacks are commonly mistaken for heart attacks because of how similar they act.

Depression, a complex and multifaceted mental health condition, has seen a notable increase in awareness and destigmatization. Public figures and celebrities have played a crucial role in normalizing conversations about depression, helping dispel misconceptions, and fostering an environment of empathy and support. Efforts to improve access to mental health services have been underway, making it easier for individuals to seek professional help and find appropriate treatment options. Depression still has a stigmatism especially when society feels that it is misrepresented for an overdiagnosed for the blues. Depression is an empty hole deep within your soul. It is much greater than feeling sad and if untreated it could have lasting effects on the person for the rest of their life.

The acknowledgment of the interconnectedness between mental and physical health has also gained prominence in the past decade. Recognizing that mental health impacts day-to-day lives extends beyond emotional well-being to influence physical health, productivity, and overall quality of life. Employers, educators, and healthcare providers have increasingly embraced holistic approaches to well-being, understanding that mental health is not isolated but intricately linked with other facets of life.

Technology has played a significant role in advancing mental health awareness and support. Mobile applications, online resources, and telehealth services have become valuable tools in providing information, self-help resources, and remote access to mental health professionals. These innovations have helped bridge gaps in accessibility and reduce barriers to seeking mental health care.

Treat and Control Your Mental Health

In the pursuit of mental well-being, adopting proactive strategies is essential to treat and control various aspects of mental health.

Recognizing the interconnected nature of physical and mental health, individuals can implement a range of practices and seek various supports to foster a balanced and resilient state of mind.

One foundational pillar of mental health maintenance is regular exercise. Physical activity has been shown to have a positive impact on mood by promoting the release of endorphins, the body's natural mood lifters. Engaging in activities like walking, jogging, or yoga not only contributes to physical fitness but also serves as an effective means of stress reduction. Additionally, exercise provides a structured outlet for pent-up energy and tension, promoting a sense of accomplishment and well-being.

Mindfulness and meditation practices have gained widespread recognition for their effectiveness in managing mental health. Mindfulness involves cultivating a heightened awareness of the present moment, allowing individuals to observe their thoughts without judgment. Meditation, whether guided or self-directed, can aid in reducing stress, anxiety, and promoting emotional regulation. Incorporating mindfulness into daily routines through practices like deep breathing exercises or mindful eating can contribute to long-term mental well-being.

Professional mental health support is a crucial component of treatment and control. Some Mental Health is best left with the professionals. Psychotherapy, or talk therapy, provides individuals with a safe space to explore and address their thoughts, feelings, and behaviors. Cognitive-behavioral therapy is one such approach that focuses on identifying and modifying negative thought patterns and behaviors. Therapeutic interventions offer tailored strategies for managing specific mental health concerns, providing individuals with coping mechanisms and tools to navigate life's challenges.

Pharmacological interventions, such as medications prescribed by mental health professionals, can be beneficial in certain cases, but always remember to check with your doctor and your psychiatrist. Antidepressants, anxiolytics, and mood stabilizers are examples of medications that may be prescribed to address specific mental health conditions. It is essential, however, for individuals to work closely with healthcare providers to monitor medication effectiveness, and potential side effects, and adjust treatment plans as needed. Medication should only be taken for severe symptoms or physically incapable of controlling your emotions.

Social support plays a pivotal role in maintaining and improving mental health. Strong connections with friends, family, and a supportive community contribute to a sense of belonging and reduce feelings of isolation. Engaging in social activities, fostering positive relationships, and seeking emotional support during challenging times are integral components of building a robust support system. Those bonds also help regarding a shoulder to lean on. These people understand you and your struggles and can provide an ear to listen and help you. It is not as unbiased as a therapist, but it can be more personal.

Healthy lifestyle choices, including proper nutrition and adequate sleep, significantly impact mental health.

Nutrient-rich diets that support brain function, coupled with consistent and restorative sleep patterns, contribute to overall well-being. Prioritizing self-care and setting healthy boundaries to manage stressors are crucial aspects of maintaining a balanced and sustainable lifestyle. This also includes certain foods or beverages that may be used as comfort foods during stress. Don't try and run to these options every time as it creates an addiction to relieve pain which will be discussed later in the book.

Embracing hobbies and activities that bring joy and fulfillment can enhance mental well-being. Whether it's creative pursuits, sports, or spending time in nature, engaging in activities that align with personal interests promotes a positive outlook and provides a constructive outlet for emotional expression. Hobbies truly can make a difference in your mental health. It helps us do things that make us feel unique while also being a relaxing way to settle our minds.

<u>What You Aim to Become</u>

Now that you know yourself and what makes you tick, it is time to put into plan on what you want to become. This is not a statement to stop or replace your personality and traits, but to focus on things that need improvement. For example, if you are known for having the last word, try instead to leave the sentence where it is and think about what was spoken. Here are some examples that can be helpful:

1. Before responding to a colleague's suggestion in a meeting, take a moment to pause and consider the impact of your words. Mindfully choose language that is constructive rather than dismissive to foster a positive and collaborative atmosphere.

1. If facing a challenging project deadline, instead of expressing frustration and cynicism, employ cognitive-behavioral techniques. Challenge negative thoughts like "This is impossible" and reframe them with statements like "I can break this down into manageable tasks."

1. If recurrent anger issues are affecting relationships, consider seeking therapy. A therapist can provide strategies to address underlying triggers and develop healthier responses, promoting more positive interactions with others.

1. After a stressful day at work, engage in a physical activity like jogging or yoga. Physical exercise can help release pent-up tension, providing a healthier outlet for stress and reducing the likelihood of taking frustrations out on others.

1. When feeling overwhelmed by stress, confide in a friend or family member. Sharing concerns can alleviate anxiety and provide a fresh perspective, fostering emotional support and understanding.

1. When a frustrating situation arises, take a moment to identify the source of anger before reacting. Acknowledge the emotion and communicate assertively, rather than letting anger dictate responses and potentially damage a relationship.

1. Establish clear boundaries with friends or colleagues to manage expectations. Communicate openly about time constraints and avoid overcommitting, preventing undue stress and potential conflicts.

1. Regularly reflect on communication patterns and interpersonal interactions. Set realistic goals for improvement, such as consciously choosing words that uplift and empower others, and celebrate progress along the way.

These are just some small examples of things that might arise, but the more you mitigate your actions and feelings when confronting individuals and others. You should also implement a more positive approach in your everyday life. The more positive you are every day the more minimal things seem to not matter or can be easily fixed. The more uncontrolled your emotions become the higher the chance for the situation to become worse. So to do better we must be better and take control of our emotions so that they are not making the choices for us.

Chapter 6: Relationships

Building and maintaining relationships is a fundamental aspect of human existence, contributing significantly to our emotional, psychological, and social well-being. Relationships provide a sense of belonging, support, and connection, playing a crucial role in shaping our identity and overall happiness. They offer a framework for individuals to share experiences, navigate challenges, and find meaning in their lives.

Friendship is a cornerstone of social relationships, characterized by mutual affection, trust, and shared interests. Friends offer companionship, understanding, and a support system that can be vital during difficult times. These relationships are often voluntary, based on personal choice and compatibility. Friendships contribute to emotional resilience, as individuals can confide in their friends and seek advice, fostering a sense of belonging and camaraderie.

Family bonds are something you inherently are born or raised into. Individuals raised in a family form a bond with those within their family that connects them as a unit and groups them into separate families. These relationships are formed at a very young age and share support, a loving environment, and a synergistic form of living together.

Work relationships are an integral part of professional life, playing a pivotal role in career development and job satisfaction. Colleagues collaborate to achieve common goals, share knowledge, and create a positive work environment. Strong work relationships can enhance productivity, boost morale, and create a sense of teamwork.

Additionally, these connections often extend beyond the workplace, providing opportunities for personal growth and networking.

Romantic relationships represent a unique and complex form of connection, characterized by emotional intimacy, shared goals, and physical attraction. These relationships contribute to personal development, allowing individuals to learn about themselves and their partners. Romantic bonds can provide emotional support, companionship, and a foundation for building a family. However, they also require effective communication, trust, and compromise to thrive. Relationships provide a sense of purpose and fulfillment. Human beings are inherently social creatures, and meaningful connections contribute to a sense of community and shared experiences. In times of joy or sorrow, having a support system enhances one's ability to cope with life's challenges. Shared memories, experiences, and achievements create a tapestry of connection that adds richness and depth to our lives.

Positive Relationships

Positive relationships, regardless of their nature, share common traits that contribute to a fulfilling and enriching experience.

In friendships, a positive relationship is characterized by mutual trust, respect, and genuine companionship. Friends support each other's individual growth, celebrate successes, and offer comfort during challenging times. Open communication is key, allowing friends to share thoughts and feelings freely, fostering understanding, and deepening the bond. Positive friendships contribute to a sense of belonging and provide emotional sustenance, enhancing overall well-being.

In family relationships, positivity thrives on unconditional love, acceptance, and support. Healthy family dynamics involve effective communication, where members feel heard and understood. Respect for each other's autonomy and differences is crucial, fostering an environment of trust and cooperation. Positive family relationships contribute to emotional stability, a sense of identity, and a lifelong support system. They create a foundation that empowers individuals to navigate life's challenges with resilience and confidence.

Romantic relationships thrive on intimacy, communication, and shared goals. A positive romantic relationship involves mutual respect, trust, and emotional connection. Partners support each other's personal and professional aspirations, fostering an environment where both individuals can grow and evolve. Effective communication ensures that concerns are addressed, conflicts are resolved, and the relationship deepens over time. Positivity in romantic relationships enhances emotional well-being, providing a secure and loving space for personal and shared experiences.

Work relationships characterized by positivity contribute to a healthy and productive professional environment. Colleagues who communicate openly, respect each other's contributions and collaborate effectively create a positive workplace culture. Supportive work relationships boost morale, motivation, and job satisfaction. Positive professional connections not only improve the quality of work but also contribute to career advancement and personal growth, creating a fulfilling and rewarding professional life. Expectations in positive relationships include active listening, empathy, and a commitment to mutual growth. Healthy relationships involve a balance of give and take, where both parties contribute to the well-being of the connection. Positive relationships require effort, understanding, and the ability to navigate challenges together. They provide a sense of security, foster personal development, and contribute to an overall sense of happiness and fulfillment.

The benefits of positive relationships extend beyond immediate emotional satisfaction. Research consistently shows that individuals with strong social connections tend to lead healthier lives. Positive relationships can contribute to lower stress levels, improved mental health, and even physical well-being. In times of crisis or joy, having a network of positive relationships offers a support system that enhances one's ability to cope with life's complexities.

Negative Relationships

Negative and harmful relationships can manifest in various forms, leaving a detrimental impact on individuals' well-being and overall quality of life.

In family dynamics, a negative relationship might be characterized by persistent conflict, lack of support, and emotional toxicity. Signs of such relationships include frequent arguments, manipulation, or the presence of abusive behaviors. Family members may feel trapped in a cycle of negativity, experiencing stress, anxiety, and emotional distress due to the unhealthy dynamics within the family unit.

In friendships, negative relationships can exhibit traits such as betrayal, envy, and a lack of trust. Signs of a harmful friendship include constant criticism, gossip, or a one-sided dynamic where one person consistently takes advantage of the other. A toxic friendship can erode self-esteem, create feelings of isolation, and hinder personal growth. Recognizing signs of negativity in friendships is crucial for preserving mental and emotional well-being.

Work relationships tainted by negativity can impede professional growth and job satisfaction. Signs of a negative work relationship may include a lack of collaboration, unresolved conflicts, or a toxic work environment. Instances of bullying, harassment, or undermining behavior can be indicative of harmful professional relationships. Such negativity can lead to stress, decreased productivity, and a decline in overall job satisfaction, affecting both mental and physical health.

In romantic relationships, negativity can manifest through various forms of abuse, including emotional, verbal, or physical abuse. Signs of a harmful romantic relationship may include controlling behavior, isolation from friends and family, or a consistent pattern of disrespect. Individuals in such relationships may experience fear, anxiety, and a compromised sense of self-worth.

Recognizing these signs is crucial for breaking free from the cycle of abuse and seeking support. Common signs of negative relationships across all categories include a lack of effective communication, an imbalance of power, and the absence of mutual respect. When communication becomes hostile or non-existent, when power dynamics are skewed, and when respect is consistently lacking, relationships are more likely to become harmful. These signs can often serve as red flags, signaling the need for reflection, intervention, and potentially, the decision to distance oneself from the negative relationship.

How to Improve Your Relationships

Improving a relationship requires intentional effort, open communication, and a commitment to fostering trust and respect. Key factors such as trust, communication, and respect form the foundation for building and strengthening relationships. Implementing strategies to enhance these factors in real-life scenarios can lead to more fulfilling and harmonious connections.

Trust is a fundamental aspect of any healthy relationship. To build trust, it's essential to be reliable and consistent in your actions. For example, if you promise to do something, follow through on your commitment. Consistency creates a sense of predictability and reliability, contributing to the development of trust. Additionally, being transparent and honest in your communication helps to establish trust. Openly share your thoughts and feelings, and encourage your partner or friend to do the same. By being transparent, you create an environment where trust can flourish. An example of trust would be being vulnerable and sharing your emotions, reinforcing the emotional bond between partners, or confiding in an individual with things that matter to you.

Communication is the cornerstone of successful relationships. Active listening is a crucial component of effective communication. When engaged in a conversation, focus on understanding the other person's perspective rather than just waiting for your turn to speak. Reflective listening, where you repeat or paraphrase what the other person has said, demonstrates that you are truly trying to comprehend their point of view. Furthermore, using "I" statements instead of "you" statements can prevent defensive reactions and foster a more collaborative and understanding dialogue. An example of this is saying " You need to clean the house it's messy" vs " I feel frustrated coming home when the house is messy". It opens up a more open dialogue for the solution to be fixed instead of blaming someone for the way the home looks.

Respect is a key factor that contributes to a positive and healthy relationship. One practical way to demonstrate respect is by acknowledging and appreciating differences. Recognize that individuals have unique perspectives, preferences, and boundaries. Avoid making assumptions and take the time to understand and appreciate the diversity within the relationship. Additionally, respecting personal boundaries is crucial. Ask for consent before sharing personal information or offering advice, and be mindful of the other person's comfort levels.

In a romantic relationship, trust, communication, and respect can be actively improved through regular check-ins and quality time together. Schedule dedicated time for meaningful conversations, away from distractions, to discuss feelings, goals, and concerns. Participate in activities that you both enjoy to strengthen your connection and create shared experiences.

. In a workplace, effective communication is vital for collaboration and team dynamics. Regular team meetings can provide a platform for open communication, allowing team members to share updates, express concerns, and offer feedback. Acknowledging and celebrating achievements, both individual and collective, fosters a positive work environment and reinforces mutual respect. Providing constructive feedback respectfully is essential for professional growth and team cohesion. In friendships, strengthening trust and communication involves being supportive and available. Listen when your friend needs to talk and offer empathy and understanding. Respect their boundaries and choices, even if they differ from your own. Being there for your friends during both challenging and celebratory times builds a foundation of trust and reinforces the importance of the relationship.

<u>Ending a Relationship</u>

Ending a relationship is a challenging and often emotionally charged process, but there are situations where it becomes necessary for the mental health and well-being of the individuals involved. Recognizing when a relationship has turned negative and is adversely impacting one's mental health is a crucial step toward making a difficult decision. Negative relationships can manifest in various forms, including constant conflict, emotional abuse, or a lack of support. In these circumstances, choosing to separate oneself from the relationship is an act of self-preservation and an acknowledgment of the importance of prioritizing mental health.

While the decision to end a relationship may initially feel wrong or difficult, it is essential to recognize the long-term benefits. The negative impact of a toxic relationship on mental health can be profound, leading to increased stress, anxiety, and even depression. By choosing to end such a relationship, individuals create space for personal growth, healing, and the pursuit of a healthier and more positive life. It is crucial to prioritize one's mental well-being, even if it means making a tough decision to sever ties with a relationship that has become detrimental. It's important to note that ending a relationship doesn't necessarily mean burning bridges permanently.

In some cases, taking a break or creating distance can be an opportunity for both individuals to reflect, grow independently, and potentially address the underlying issues that contributed to the negativity. If both parties are willing to work on themselves and make necessary changes, there is a possibility of repairing the relationship down the road. This could involve seeking therapy, engaging in open and honest communication, and committing to positive changes for the benefit of both individuals.

The aftermath of ending a relationship requires a period of self-reflection and self-care. Individuals may experience a range of emotions, including grief, relief, or even guilt. It's essential to allow oneself the time and space to process these emotions and seek support from friends, family, or mental health professionals. Engaging in activities that promote personal well-being, such as exercise, hobbies, or therapy, can contribute to the healing process and aid in moving forward.

Communication is key when ending a relationship, and it's important to express one's feelings and reasons with honesty and empathy. Clearly communicating the decision, while being respectful and considerate of the other person's emotions, can facilitate a more understanding and amicable separation. However, it's crucial to prioritize one's mental health and set necessary boundaries to ensure a healthy and supportive post-breakup environment. By following everything regarding the relationship discussed above it will help you make stronger bonds and remove those that have been negative will make a difference regarding those around you and your way of living.

Chapter 7: Addiction

Everyone has heard of addiction being tossed around, but what is addiction really? At the heart of addiction lies the intricate dance of neurotransmitters within the brain. Dopamine, a neurotransmitter associated with pleasure and reward, plays a central role in the development of addictive behaviors. When exposed to substances like drugs or engaging in rewarding activities such as gambling, the brain's reward system releases a surge of dopamine. This surge reinforces the behavior, creating a positive association and motivating individuals to seek out the substance or behavior again. Over time, the brain adapts to the increased dopamine levels, leading to a diminished response and prompting individuals to escalate their consumption or engagement to achieve the same level of pleasure.

The evolutionary roots of addiction can be traced back to the survival instincts of our ancestors. The reward system in the brain, designed to reinforce beneficial behaviors like eating and procreation, inadvertently makes individuals susceptible to the allure of addictive substances and behaviors. In prehistoric times, seeking out high-calorie foods or engaging in risk-taking behaviors could confer a survival advantage. However, in the modern world, this reward system can be hijacked by substances like drugs or behaviors like compulsive gambling, leading to maladaptive patterns that compromise individual well-being.

Genetics also play a crucial role in predisposing individuals to addiction. Twin and family studies have consistently shown a heritable component in addictive behaviors. Specific genetic variations can influence how individuals respond to substances and their susceptibility to developing addictive tendencies. Understanding these genetic factors not only sheds light on the heritability of addiction but also provides potential targets for preventive interventions and personalized treatment approaches.

While genetics sets the stage, environmental factors contribute significantly to the development of addiction. Stress, trauma, and socioeconomic conditions can exacerbate susceptibility to addictive behaviors. Additionally, societal attitudes and accessibility to addictive substances play a pivotal role. Cultural norms and social pressures can either amplify or mitigate the risk of addiction, shaping individual behaviors within a broader societal context.

One prominent factor contributing to the surge in addiction is the rapid evolution of technology. The accessibility of smartphones, social media, and online platforms has introduced new avenues for instant gratification. Social media platforms, in particular, create an environment where validation, comparison, and the pursuit of constant stimuli can become addictive. The constant barrage of notifications and the allure of a digital world at our fingertips can lead individuals to seek solace and escape through addictive behaviors, such as excessive screen time, gaming, or compulsive internet use.

The modern world operates at a relentless pace, exposing individuals to unprecedented levels of stress and overstimulation. The demands of work, family, and social obligations can create an environment where individuals turn to substances like alcohol, prescription medications, or illicit drugs as coping mechanisms. The pressure to excel and the fear of missing out contribute to a heightened vulnerability to addictive behaviors as people search for ways to alleviate stress and find momentary relief.

Types of Addiction

Addiction, traditionally associated with substance use disorders, has evolved to encompass a broad spectrum of behaviors that extend beyond chemical dependencies. Let's talk about shedding light on non-substance-related compulsions that impact individuals across diverse facets of life. From technology to gambling, these addictive behaviors share common underlying mechanisms that can have profound effects on mental health and well-being.

1. Substance Addiction

The most recognized form of addiction involves substances such as alcohol, tobacco, and illicit drugs. These substances hijack the brain's reward system, leading to compulsive use despite adverse consequences. Substance use disorders not only affect physical health but also have far-reaching social and psychological implications, often requiring comprehensive treatment approaches for recovery. Because the substances provide a temporary high, most people use these substances at an alarming amount crossing over into addiction and turning to harder and more severe substances and usage.

1. Technology Addiction

THIS IS A NEW FORM of addiction that has been on the rise since the big internet boom. Individuals may find themselves compulsively checking social media, playing video games, or engaging in online activities to the detriment of real-world responsibilities. Technology addiction shares neurobiological similarities with substance addiction, as both involve the release of dopamine in the brain's reward pathways.

1. Gambling Addiction

Gambling addiction, or ludomania, is another non-substance-related disorder characterized by an uncontrollable urge to gamble despite negative consequences. The thrill of risk and the anticipation of reward triggers the release of neurotransmitters, creating a cycle of reinforcement that can lead to financial ruin and strained relationships.

1. **Food Addiction**

Food addiction involves the compulsive consumption of certain foods, often high in sugar, fat, or salt, despite negative health consequences. The pleasure derived from eating triggers the release of dopamine, creating a reward cycle similar to that seen in substance addictions. This behavior can contribute to obesity and associated health issues. This addiction goes beyond the range of eating comfort foods and gorging yourself to the extreme.

1. **Shopping Addiction**

Compulsive shopping, often fueled by consumerism and materialism, can develop into a form of addiction. The act of making purchases and the associated anticipation of acquiring new possessions activate the brain's reward system, leading to a cycle of impulsive buying despite financial strain.

There are plenty more addictions that are not listed, but there are many similarities to all of these addictions. There will be a financial strain, a negative impact on your relationships, and a negative impact on your mental health. Addiction can start as something that seems harmless, but the more you do it, the less the dopamine kicks in making you need to increase it in dosage, timespan, and consistency causing users of any addiction to negate every aspect of their lives ultimately making you a worse version of yourself.

Why We Get Addicted

YOU MAY ASK YOURSELF why we get addicted or why you don't get addicted and others do when doing the same thing and there are a few key factors as to why that is. One of the primary contributors to addiction lies in the aftermath of trauma. Individuals who have experienced physical, emotional, or psychological trauma may turn to substances or behaviors as a coping mechanism. Trauma can disrupt the normal functioning of the brain, influencing the reward pathways and making individuals more susceptible to the allure of substances that provide temporary relief from the pain and distress associated with their traumatic experiences. Trauma can be from the smallest things such as a break up to large things like the loss of a loved one. Trauma affects each and every one of us and those who can not bear the pain in their heart seek something to numb said pain so that they do not feel it anymore. This becomes a vicious cycle without the trauma ever being addressed and the issue becoming more and more big as it snowballs to self-destruction.

Another key factor is escapism. The desire to escape from the challenges and pressures of reality is a powerful motivator for addictive behaviors. Whether it's the numbing effects of drugs and alcohol, the immersive escape of video games, or the thrill of risky behaviors, the quest for an altered state of consciousness is often driven by the need to temporarily disconnect from life itself. Escapism and Trauma go hand-in-hand when addiction is in play. Escapism serves as a negative coping strategy allowing individuals to momentarily evade their problems instead of addressing them head-on. This destructive behavior also involves isolation and disconnection of relationships causing more suffering and no supportive system to help the individual.

On the other side of the coin, Negative peer groups can also affect this. It is believed that the cause of peer pressure is what causes those to succumb to addiction, but that's shifting the blame onto another instead of taking action of one's self. Social dynamics and the influence of peers can significantly contribute to the development of addictive behaviors. Individuals may be swayed by the actions and choices of those in their social circles by seeking acceptance or wanting to be involved with the group. As they say " Birds of a feather stick together.". Negative influences, such as friends engaged in substance abuse or unhealthy behaviors, can create an environment conducive to the initiation and perpetuation of addictive patterns.

Addiction often serves as a deceptive crutch, providing individuals with a temporary burst of self-worth or pleasure. The neurochemical changes that occur during substance use or engaging in addictive behaviors can create a false sense of well-being, reinforcing the belief that these actions contribute positively to one's identity.

However, this illusion of self-worth is fleeting and can lead to a dangerous cycle where individuals continually return to addictive behaviors in a misguided pursuit of long-term happiness.

How to Stop Addiction

There are many groups and programs on how to separate yourself from your addiction thanks to the rise of acknowledging mental health and a better understanding of what addiction is. These groups have varying ways to help you, but the key factors bottle down into a few things.

Acknowledgment of Wrongdoings:

The first crucial step in overcoming addiction is acknowledging the existence of the problem. Acceptance paves the way for self-reflection and a genuine commitment to change. Individuals must confront the impact of their addictive behaviors on themselves and those around them. Most addicts speak about hitting rock bottom which was their eye opener allowing them to see what they have been doing wrong and finding the courage to change. This self-awareness is the foundation upon which successful recovery can be built.

Understanding Root Causes:

To effectively address addiction, individuals must delve into the underlying causes of their behavior. This involves exploring past traumas, emotional triggers, or unmet needs that may have contributed to the development of addictive patterns. Professional therapy and counseling can be instrumental in facilitating this understanding, helping individuals identify and address the root causes of their addiction.

Implementing Cessation Methods:

Once the causes are understood, the next step is to implement effective cessation methods. This may involve seeking medical assistance for withdrawal symptoms, participating in evidence-based therapy such as cognitive-behavioral therapy, or joining support groups tailored to the specific addiction. Cessation methods should be personalized to the individual's needs and may include a combination of medical, psychological, and social interventions.

The ideal cessation methods are consistent, strict, and supportive. The more the procedure is done the more you will follow through with it. The more strict the method the less likely to return to the addiction. The best though, is the support in which someone the individual can lean on as support through their period of withdrawal, anger, sadness, and guilt.

BUILDING SUPPORTIVE Networks:

Accountability and emotional support are vital components of addiction recovery. Joining supportive groups, such as 12-step programs or therapy groups, provides individuals with a community that understands their struggles. Establishing connections with others on the same journey fosters a sense of belonging and encourages mutual accountability. Having a reliable support system, whether it's friends, family, or a sponsor, provides a crucial lifeline during challenging moments. Recovering addicts state that the biggest help to recovery was the people waiting for them at the end and being there for them on the journey.

Preventing Addiction

Being addicted falls on a small portion of humanity, but is so easy for anyone to become addicted to anything. The best way to prevent it from happening to you is to set up things along the way to protect yourself.

Genetic Awareness:

Understanding one's genetic predisposition to addiction is a key component of prevention. Genetic factors can play a significant role in susceptibility to certain substances or behaviors. Individuals with a family history of addiction may benefit from early awareness and proactive measures to mitigate risks. Genetic testing and counseling can provide valuable insights, empowering individuals to make informed decisions about their lifestyle choices.

Positive Peer Influence:

Positive peer groups significantly contribute to preventing addiction. Surrounding oneself with individuals who prioritize healthy behaviors and positive choices creates a supportive environment. Peer influence can act as a protective factor, steering individuals away from situations that may trigger addictive behaviors. Engaging in activities with like-minded individuals fosters a sense of community and reinforces positive lifestyle choices.

Moderation Practices:

Practicing moderation is a fundamental preventive strategy. Encouraging individuals to establish balanced and sustainable habits reduces the likelihood of developing addictive tendencies. This involves cultivating awareness of consumption patterns, setting boundaries, and maintaining a healthy balance between work, social life, and personal well-being. This can easily be seen as an example of alcohol consumption. Alcohol is a beverage all individuals drink in the world. The key to moderation is to set limits and amounts of when you should or shouldn't drink as it can easily become a slippery slope.

Addiction can be a very deadly beast with critical negative effects on your entire life. Even the strongest person can succumb to addiction without the right protection and preventative matters. If you are addicted to something and can see it, you have to take that first step above all. Remember " A person in motion stays in motion". The more you focus on recovering the more likely you are to complete it. Never give up on the struggle even if you falter. Find something dear to you that you can cling on to keep you on the right path. For those tilting towards addiction, it is never too late to stop before it becomes a problem. See the signs and make changes so that you don't face the deadly beast. With all this, you can do better and be better.

Chapter 8: Job

In contemporary society, the role of employment extends far beyond merely providing financial sustenance; it serves as a cornerstone for personal growth, self-esteem, and societal stability. This two-fold significance of jobs underscores their importance for both individuals and the broader community.

For an individual, a job is more than a means of earning a livelihood; it is a pathway to personal development and self-actualization. Employment fosters a sense of purpose and accomplishment, as individuals contribute their skills and efforts to the accomplishment of organizational goals. Through work, individuals often discover and hone their talents, develop critical thinking skills, and acquire valuable experience. This continuous learning process not only enhances one's professional expertise but also contributes to personal growth, fostering a well-rounded and resilient individual.

Moreover, a job provides a crucial foundation for a person's sense of identity and self-esteem. Employment allows individuals to define themselves in the context of their contributions to the workplace and society. The inherent value of one's work can lead to a heightened sense of self-worth, promoting mental and emotional well-being. The structure and routine of employment also contribute to a sense of stability and purpose, mitigating feelings of aimlessness and uncertainty that can arise in the absence of meaningful occupation.

Beyond the individual, the societal implications of employment are profound. Gainful employment plays a pivotal role in maintaining social order and stability. When a significant portion of the population is employed, it reduces the likelihood of social unrest and fosters a sense of shared responsibility. Gainful employment contributes to the overall economic health of a society, as a productive and engaged workforce fuels innovation, economic growth, and competitiveness on a global scale.

Furthermore, employment is a powerful tool for reducing poverty and inequality. Meaningful employment opportunities provide individuals with a means to lift themselves out of poverty, promoting social mobility and equalizing opportunities. Additionally, gainful employment is closely tied to social cohesion. It fosters a sense of community and shared purpose, as individuals collaborate to achieve common objectives. The workplace often serves as a microcosm of society, promoting diversity, inclusion, and the exchange of ideas.

Through these interactions, individuals learn to navigate differences, fostering a more tolerant and cohesive society.

A well-functioning society relies on a diverse array of professions, each playing a unique role in maintaining its stability and vitality. Healthcare professionals, including doctors and nurses, are indispensable for the well-being of individuals, managing illnesses, and promoting preventive care. Teachers and educators shape the intellectual and social development of future generations, forming a cornerstone of societal progress. First responders, such as police officers and firefighters, are crucial for public safety, ensuring the maintenance of law and order during crises. Infrastructure workers, including civil engineers and construction crews, provide the physical framework for daily life, building and maintaining roads, bridges, and utilities. Technology professionals, from IT specialists to cybersecurity experts, contribute to information flow, system security, and technological advancements that propel society forward.

Agricultural workers, encompassing farmers and agricultural scientists, ensure a stable food supply, addressing a fundamental need of the population. Transportation workers, such as truck drivers and pilots, facilitate the movement of goods and people, connecting regions and nations to support trade and the global economy. Environmental conservationists, through their work in environmental science and conservation, protect natural resources and promote sustainability for the benefit of future generations. Retail and service workers, including salespeople and customer service representatives, contribute to the economy by providing goods and services that meet the population's diverse needs.

Social workers and counselors provide critical support to individuals and families facing challenges, promoting mental and emotional well-being. Scientists and researchers contribute to societal advancement through breakthroughs in medicine, technology, and a deeper understanding of the world. Government officials and administrators, along with civil servants, create and implement policies that govern society, ensuring order, justice, and the protection of citizens' rights. Media and communication professionals, including journalists and editors, play a crucial role in informing the public, shaping opinions, and fostering transparency. Manufacturing workers, from factory workers to production line managers, contribute to the production of goods that satisfy the needs and desires of society. Together, these diverse roles form the intricate tapestry of a well-functioning society, where each profession, despite its differences, is indispensable for overall stability, progress, and quality of life.

<u>What Job do you Want?</u>

We know that jobs are important to society and the vast variety of each job varies significantly, but what do you want as a job? Embarking on a journey to find the right career is a profound and often introspective process that requires careful consideration, self-reflection, and strategic planning. In a world of diverse professional opportunities, identifying the right career path is not just about financial gain but also personal fulfillment, alignment with values, and a sense of purpose. To navigate this intricate journey successfully, individuals must embark on a thoughtful exploration of their skills, interests, values, and aspirations.

At the heart of the quest for the right career lies self-discovery. Understanding one's skills and strengths is important. Individuals should take stock of their academic achievements, practical skills, and innate talents. This introspective process involves recognizing both hard skills, such as technical expertise, and soft skills, such as communication or problem-solving abilities. It is crucial to identify areas where personal aptitude intersects with professional potential. The more keen you are with certain skills the easier the job will be. When you find the job the clicks its as if a piece of the puzzle has connected perfectly.

Equally significant is an exploration of personal interests. Passion is often the driving force behind career satisfaction. By reflecting on hobbies, favorite subjects, and activities that bring joy, individuals can uncover potential career paths that resonate with their genuine interests. For instance, someone with a penchant for creativity might find fulfillment in a career in graphic design or writing, while a natural problem solver might thrive in a role that involves analytical thinking and strategic planning. Hobbies can even evolve into a career if you put work into the hobby and have a solid plan for a stable income.

Values also play a pivotal role in career alignment. An individual's core beliefs, ethics, and principles should harmonize with the ethos of their chosen profession. A career that aligns with personal values not only fosters a sense of fulfillment but also ensures ethical decision-making and sustained motivation in the face of challenges. Whether it's a commitment to social justice, environmental sustainability, or innovation, understanding these values provides a compass for navigating the professional landscape. Be careful though, as some careers reveal a hidden value alignment that doesn't fit with yours and could make the job feel as though it wasn't what you seemed.

Furthermore, aspirations and long-term goals should be considered. A successful career is not static but evolves over time. As individuals grow and change, so too should their career aspirations. Setting realistic short-term and long-term goals can guide the trajectory of a career, providing milestones for professional development and personal growth. Regularly reassessing these goals allows for adjustments in response to changing circumstances or evolving passions. This will be discussed later in the chapter regarding stepping stones to your finish goal.

Practical experience and exposure are invaluable in the pursuit of the right career. Internships, informational interviews, and networking events provide opportunities to gain insights into various industries, connect with professionals, and test the waters before making a definitive career choice. Internships, in particular, offer hands-on experience, allowing individuals to gauge whether a specific field aligns with their expectations and preferences. Hands-on work that you can be a part of or observe is the best format for learning a career you want to do. It is heavily applied to not only do research, but try and reach out to someone that does the job so that you can get an inside look at what you would do and how it is done.

While self-reflection is foundational, seeking guidance from mentors, career counselors, and professionals in the chosen field can provide valuable perspectives. Mentors, with their wealth of experience, can offer insights into the realities of different professions, share personal anecdotes, and guide navigating potential challenges. Networking with professionals through informational interviews or industry events can broaden one's understanding of various career paths and create valuable connections for future opportunities. This form of learning is great for those seeking to open up their own business or entrepreneurial lines of work. Having someone who has done it already and can better guide you on what you should or shouldn't do is extremely important and helpful in the long run as the people you speak to have seen the pitfalls ahead and have survived on the other side.

Reaching the End Goal

In order to reach the end goal first you need to meet the requirements for the job. If it involves schooling, a degree, or apprenticeship, most jobs will not hire until those said requirements are met. These skills take time so be patient when you choose what you want to do. The next step is getting ready to apply for the job.

The job application process is a critical juncture in one's professional journey, demanding a strategic approach to maximize chances of success. It begins with a compelling resume and a tailored cover letter that perfectly highlights one's skills, experiences, and enthusiasm for the position. The resume should be meticulously written, emphasizing achievements, relevant qualifications, and a clear career trajectory. Additionally, a well-crafted cover letter provides an opportunity to articulate one's interest in the role, showcasing an understanding of the company's values and goals. Tailoring application materials to the specific job and company demonstrates genuine interest and attention to detail, setting a positive tone. You can also reach out personally to the hiring party to let them know about your submission of your resume and cover letter. Taking that extra step shows how much you are interested and ready to work for the company.

As technology continues to reshape the job application landscape, leveraging online platforms is crucial. Many employers use applicant tracking systems to screen resumes, emphasizing the need for keywords and clean formatting. Social media profiles, especially LinkedIn, can serve as digital extensions of the resume, showcasing a professional online presence. A thoughtfully written and complete LinkedIn profile not only complements the application but also allows for networking opportunities within the industry.

Once the initial hurdle of securing an interview is cleared, the next step is to consider the appropriate attire. Dressing professionally is a reflection of respect for the opportunity and an acknowledgment of the company's culture. Understanding the industry and the company's dress code is essential. While business formal attire may be suitable for corporate settings, a more casual or creative industry may warrant a business casual approach.

Attention to grooming and personal presentation is equally vital. Cleanliness, a polished appearance, and appropriate accessories contribute to an overall professional image. A balance between style and conformity to workplace norms is key; one should aim to project competence, confidence, and cultural fit through their chosen attire.

ADVANCING WITHIN A career requires a proactive and strategic approach that extends beyond the initial job placement. Continuous learning and skill development are crucial for staying relevant and competitive. Taking advantage of training opportunities, workshops, and professional development programs can enhance both technical and soft skills, positioning an individual as an asset within their organization.

Building a strong professional network is another key element in climbing the career ladder. Actively engaging with colleagues, attending industry events, and participating in networking groups can create valuable connections. Mentoring relationships are particularly beneficial, providing guidance, insight, and a support system for career growth. Remember that you catch more flies with honey as you do not want to ruin a chance that could hurt your career down the road. Always be respectful and professional on the job.

Demonstrating initiative and a willingness to take on additional responsibilities can significantly impact career advancement. Volunteering for challenging projects, offering solutions to organizational challenges, and showcasing leadership skills can capture the attention of supervisors and open doors to new opportunities. Seeking feedback and implementing constructive criticism fosters continuous improvement and underscores a commitment to personal and professional growth. Make sure not to take too much for you to swallow as failing a project entrusted to you could have negative effects of being asked again.

Finally, effective communication is a linchpin for career progression. Articulating career goals, expressing interest in leadership roles, and maintaining transparent communication with supervisors contribute to a clear trajectory within the organization. Building a reputation for reliability, professionalism, and a positive attitude establishes a foundation for long-term success.

These are all needed, to get the job you wanted, but what happens if you finally get the job, but it isn't what you expected?

<u>Pivoting and Stepping Stones</u>

You finally got the job of your dream or so you thought. You spent multiple years in school and when you finally get to the job you realize this isn't what you wanted to do for the rest of your life. This is actually quite common and nothing to be ashamed or fearful about as most people think they wasted too much of their time already. You can either return to school for a different career using the credits to switch over that qualify or you can try a different job with the same degree. This is the form we call pivoting.

Leaving a job that no longer brings satisfaction or fulfillment can be a challenging but necessary step in one's professional journey. Whether due to a lack of growth opportunities, changing personal priorities, or a misalignment with company values, the decision to move on requires careful consideration and a strategic approach.

Before initiating the departure process, it's essential to conduct a thorough self-assessment to pinpoint the reasons behind the desire to leave. Consider whether the discontent stems from specific aspects of the job, such as the work itself, the company culture, or your growth trajectory within the organization. Understanding these factors will not only guide your decision-making but also facilitate transparent communication with your employer. This will also help when searching for a new job so you know what to avoid for the next one. Another thing is you need to have a job lined up before you begin the leaving process. If you quit your job and have nothing to go into nor any stock of money while looking, it could hurt you financially causing a lot of issues until you can stabilize with a source of income.

During the notice period, maintain your commitment to your current role and responsibilities. This period is not only a professional courtesy but also an opportunity to leave a positive final impression. Collaborate with your team to ensure a smooth handover of tasks, and document processes, and offer to assist in the training of a replacement if applicable. This proactive approach demonstrates integrity and a commitment to the team's success even as you prepare to depart. Don't leave by burning bridges as they could be used as a recommendation or collateral contact when going to another job.

LEAVING A JOB THAT no longer brings joy is also an opportunity for personal reflection and growth. Assess the skills, experiences, and insights gained during your time with the company. Reflect on what aspects of the job contributed positively to your professional development and what you hope to find in your next endeavor. This self-reflection can guide your job search and help you identify roles that align more closely with your values, aspirations, and personal satisfaction.

As you bid farewell to your current job, take proactive steps to prepare for the future. Update your resume, LinkedIn profile, and any other professional platforms. Leverage your network for job search support and potential opportunities. Consider seeking guidance from mentors or career advisors to explore new paths or industries that align better with your goals.

It's essential to approach the job search with optimism and an openness to new possibilities. Seek roles that not only match your skills but also offer a work environment and culture conducive to your professional and personal well-being. Embrace the transition as a chance for renewal and a step toward a more fulfilling and satisfying career path.

Remember that some jobs aren't meant to be the end goal careers. A lot of jobs especially at younger ages are meant to be stepping stones towards your career-ending path. These jobs are there to build up credit on how well you perform a job, working with other individuals, working with customers, and preparing you on how to be professional and follow a working schedule. Trying out different jobs at a young age can pay off to find that one job that fits you and it's understandable to try out different jobs in variety. Remember if you can find a job that you love or currently working towards, it will be better in the long run.

Chapter 9: Goals and Dreams

Achievable goals are the cornerstone of personal success, providing a clear roadmap for individuals seeking self-improvement. These goals are characterized by their realism, feasibility, and relevance to personal aspirations. Crafted with a practical understanding of one's capabilities, resources, and time constraints, achievable goals empower individuals to make tangible strides in various aspects of their lives.

For the average person, setting achievable goals is not only beneficial but also essential in creating a sense of direction and purpose. These goals are not mere wishful thinking; instead, they are grounded in a practical assessment of what can be realistically accomplished. By being specific and measurable, achievable goals offer a concrete framework for progress, allowing individuals to track their success and make necessary adjustments along the way.

In health and fitness, an achievable goal could be to engage in regular physical activity, such as walking for at least 30 minutes five days a week. This goal is realistic, setting a specific duration and frequency that makes it easier to incorporate into a busy schedule. Walking, a low-impact exercise, promotes overall well-being.

For professional development, an achievable goal might be to attend one industry-related workshop or seminar within the next three months. This goal is feasible, focusing on a specific professional development activity with a defined timeline. Attending a workshop provides an opportunity for skill enhancement and networking.

In terms of financial stability, an achievable goal could involve saving a specific percentage of income each month towards an emergency fund. This goal is attainable, with a clear, quantifiable target for saving that promotes financial responsibility and establishes a safety net for unexpected expenses.

For education and skill enhancement, an achievable goal might involve learning a new skill, such as coding or a foreign language, by dedicating 30 minutes each day. Breaking down the learning process into manageable daily increments makes the goal achievable, emphasizing the importance of consistency in skill development.

IN PERSONAL RELATIONSHIPS, an achievable goal could be to schedule regular quality time with family or friends, such as a weekly dinner or weekend outing. This goal is realistic, emphasizing the importance of nurturing personal relationships through consistent, intentional actions.

Now goals are something that we should strive for doing better, but like every human, there are also dreams that we wish would come true. Dreams and goals are intricately woven into the fabric of human ambition, shaping the trajectory of our lives. While dreams often embody our loftiest aspirations, goals provide the pragmatic steps necessary to bring those dreams into reality. Yet, the distinction between dreams and goals is not always clear-cut, and understanding the nuanced relationship between the two is crucial for personal growth and success.

Dreams, by their nature, tend to be boundless and expansive. They are the ethereal visions that ignite our passion and imagination, reaching for the stars and pushing the boundaries of what we perceive as possible. However, dreams, when unchecked, can become dangerous. Investing heavily in an unattainable dream may lead to frustration, disappointment, and a sense of failure. It's essential to acknowledge the potential pitfalls of fixating solely on an overarching dream without a practical plan.

Conversely, goals are the tangible, measurable milestones that serve as the building blocks for realizing our dreams. Goals provide direction, structure, and a sense of purpose, breaking down the grandiosity of dreams into manageable and achievable steps. Unlike dreams, goals are grounded in reality, taking into account our current resources, capabilities, and limitations.

While it's important to recognize the potential dangers of unrestrained dreaming, it is equally crucial not to discourage the pursuit of one's dreams altogether. Dreams are the catalysts that drive innovation and progress, encouraging individuals to think beyond the ordinary and strive for the extraordinary. Instead of dismissing dreams as unattainable, a more balanced approach involves channeling the energy of dreams into a series of realistic and well-defined goals.

Leading with multiple goals can serve as a strategic and prudent approach to realizing dreams. This allows individuals to explore various avenues, adapt to changing circumstances, and mitigate the risks associated with an all-or-nothing mindset.

By diversifying goals, individuals create a flexible framework that accommodates unexpected challenges while maintaining progress toward their overarching dreams.

Consider the dream of becoming a successful entrepreneur. Instead of fixating solely on building a billion-dollar company from scratch, one could set incremental goals such as acquiring relevant skills, gaining industry experience, and networking with professionals. These goals provide practical steps that contribute to the broader dream while allowing for adjustments based on evolving circumstances.

Furthermore, the pursuit of dreams often involves a nonlinear path. Unexpected opportunities, setbacks, and personal growth experiences can shape the journey toward realizing a dream. By embracing a goal-oriented mindset, individuals can navigate these twists and turns with resilience and adaptability.

Short-Term to Long-Term

Turning short-term goals into long-term investments that manifest our dreams requires a deliberate and strategic approach. This process is akin to constructing a bridge between the present and the envisioned future. For instance, aspiring to become a professional artist is a dream that can be achieved through a series of well-crafted short-term goals. This journey involves starting with the basics, progressively refining skills, and ultimately evolving into a proficient artist capable of turning passion into a sustainable career.

Foundations: Mastering the Basics

Embarking on a journey toward a dream necessitates a solid foundation. If the dream is to become an artist, the initial short-term goals may involve learning the basics of drawing. This could include practicing fundamental techniques, understanding proportions, and experimenting with various mediums. Short-term goals at this stage are achievable and revolve around skill acquisition and exploration.

Skill Development: Gradual Complexity

As proficiency in the basics grows, short-term goals should evolve to encompass more complex challenges. For our aspiring artists, this might involve setting goals to master advanced techniques, experiment with diverse styles, or delve into digital art. Each of these short-term objectives contributes to a gradual deepening of skills and a broader understanding of the chosen craft.

Portfolio Building: Showcasing Progress

A pivotal step in the transformation of short-term goals into long-term investments is the creation of a comprehensive portfolio. Short-term goals can include producing a certain number of pieces within a specific timeframe and ensuring a diverse display of skills. This not only documents progress but also serves as a tangible representation of the journey toward the dream.

Networking and Learning: Community Engagement

Becoming a professional artist involves more than technical prowess; it requires networking and continuous learning. Short-term goals in this phase may include attending art events, joining online communities, and seeking mentorship. These objectives contribute to personal growth and provide valuable insights into the professional art world.

Monetization: Transitioning to a Career

Transforming short-term goals into long-term investments often culminates in the ability to monetize skills. For the aspiring artist, this might involve setting goals to secure the first paid commission, establish an online presence, and market services. These objectives mark the transition from a passion-driven pursuit to a sustainable and rewarding career.

Business Expansion: Scaling the Dream

Long-term dreams are not static; they can evolve and expand. Once the artist has achieved a level of success, the focus may shift to scaling the business. Goals at this stage may involve expanding the client base, diversifying services, or collaborating with other artists. This ongoing process ensures that the dream remains dynamic and aligned with personal and professional growth.

Now this is just an example of how short-term goals can stack up and become a pathway to your dreams. This process can work with many different types of dreams that can lead to things you've dreamt of coming to fruition thanks to your efforts. It will take time and the journey will be hard, but every inch forward is still a step forward toward your dream. Don't give up when things get hard and dig deep to follow that one thing that you can only dream of.

Annual and Lifetime Bucket List

Crafting dreams into reality is an art exemplified by the creation of annual and ultimate bucket lists. An annual bucket list is a dynamic compilation of short-term aspirations designed to be achieved within a single year. It acts as a roadmap, encouraging individuals to set specific, attainable goals across various facets of life, such as travel, personal development, and relationships. These time-bound objectives provide a sense of urgency and focus for the upcoming year, representing a commitment to intentional living.

On the other hand, the ultimate bucket list extends beyond the immediate future, encapsulating lifelong dreams and aspirations. This comprehensive catalogue includes deeply cherished goals, ranging from personal milestones to experiential accomplishments. It serves as a repository of desires that, when fulfilled, contribute to a profound sense of satisfaction and accomplishment throughout a lifetime.

Short-term goals, such as completing a work project or learning a new skill, can be seen as stepping stones toward the realization of annual bucket list goals. The distinction lies in the immediacy and specificity of short-term goals, addressing specific tasks within a shorter timeframe. In contrast, annual bucket list goals provide a broader view of aspirations for the upcoming year, encompassing a holistic range of objectives.

The concept of a bucket list, whether annual or ultimate, is fundamentally connected to the realization of dreams. It transcends daily routines, challenging individuals to envision a life filled with purpose and adventure. The ultimate bucket list, in particular, embodies broader dreams that shape an individual's life narrative, reminding us that life is a journey toward self-actualization rather than a mere series of tasks.

So let's take this time to personally draft up both so that they are given a solid form you can read and see every day so they don't just disappear.

Take some time to think about what you would like to do this year. Perhaps you would like to learn how to cook a certain dish or visit a certain. Whatever you choose, make sure that it is graspable within a year as that is the purpose of the annual bucket list. Next, write it all down on a sheet of paper and have it somewhere out in the open so that you can see your progress throughout the year of things you wish to accomplish. This list will help to motivate you and can be implemented into your daily or weekly schedule to help add motivation to a goal you wish to achieve. Now next take some more time to think about your dreams deeply.

What is it you want to do before the end of your life? This is where you put your wildest fantasies out so that they can also be a solid form in this world instead of only just in your dreams. There may come a time or chance for it to possibly come true and over time whether it may be a few years or even decades, go back to that list and see those dreams. Are they coming to fruition? Are they easier or harder to do? Some of those dreams might no longer even be something you want to do. The point of writing a bucket list is about something more grand and surreal than the average everyday life. It is somewhere you can dream to do and wish for what you would like to come. Never forget though that dreaming big can come with consequences, but that's what makes us human. We strive for bigger and grander things and that's okay. Because if we dream big and follow our goals we will ultimately do better.

Chapter 10: Looking Outward

In a world that thrives on diversity, the ability to comprehend and appreciate different perspectives is a fundamental skill that fosters empathy, promotes effective communication, and contributes to the building of harmonious relationships. The importance of understanding another person's perspective cannot be overstated, as it transcends individual interactions to shape the fabric of communities, societies, and the global landscape.

One of the primary reasons why it matters to know another person's perspective is the profound impact it has on empathy and compassion. When we take the time to understand the experiences, beliefs, and emotions that shape someone else's point of view, it allows us to connect with them on a deeper level. This connection lays the foundation for empathy, fostering a sense of compassion that transcends our own narrow worldview. In a world often characterized by differences, cultivating empathy becomes crucial for building bridges and fostering a sense of shared humanity.

Effective communication is the cornerstone of successful relationships, both personal and professional. Understanding another person's perspective is key to breaking down communication barriers. By grasping the nuances of their viewpoint, we can tailor our messages to be more inclusive and relatable. This not only prevents misunderstandings but also promotes a collaborative environment where diverse ideas can be shared and integrated. In the workplace, for instance, employees who appreciate their colleagues' perspectives are better equipped to work together seamlessly, leading to increased productivity and innovation.

Disagreements and conflicts are inevitable aspects of human interactions. However, understanding another person's perspective plays a pivotal role in resolving conflicts amicably. By acknowledging and respecting differing viewpoints, individuals can find common ground and work towards mutually beneficial solutions. This approach is instrumental in building harmony within families, communities, and even on a global scale. It promotes a culture of inclusivity, where diversity is celebrated rather than seen as a source of division.

As the world becomes more interconnected, cultural competence becomes increasingly essential. Understanding another person's perspective is central to developing cultural sensitivity and awareness. This awareness goes beyond mere tolerance; it involves appreciating the rich tapestry of human experiences and recognizing the value of diverse perspectives.

In a globalized society, individuals who possess cultural competence contribute to the creation of a more tolerant and inclusive world.

Understanding someone's perspective contributes significantly to personal growth by cultivating empathy and emotional intelligence. When individuals make a conscious effort to grasp the experiences and emotions that shape someone else's worldview, they develop a heightened sense of empathy. This empathetic understanding allows individuals to connect with others on a more profound level, fostering compassion and enriching their interpersonal relationships. The ability to navigate the complexities of human emotions becomes a valuable asset in personal growth, enabling individuals to forge deeper connections with a diverse range of people.

Moreover, the exposure to different perspectives acts as a catalyst for intellectual growth. Engaging with alternative viewpoints challenges preconceived notions and expands cognitive horizons. It encourages individuals to question assumptions, consider diverse ideas, and adopt a more open-minded approach to problem-solving. This intellectual flexibility not only enhances critical thinking skills but also promotes a continuous process of learning and adaptation, fostering a mindset conducive to personal development.

Observation

In the hustle and bustle of daily life, it's common for individuals to navigate their surroundings with a self-focused lens, often consumed by personal concerns and ambitions. This innate self-centeredness can significantly influence our viewpoints and decisions, limiting our ability to see the broader picture. Observing the environment and the people within it becomes a powerful tool for breaking free from this self-centric perspective, fostering a deeper understanding of the world around us.

Humans, by nature, are inclined to prioritize their experiences, needs, and desires. This self-focused tendency, while understandable, can create a distorted view of reality. It affects how we perceive others and influences the decisions we make. Taking a step back to observe the broader environment can serve as a reality check, reminding us that our individual experiences are just one part of a much larger tapestry.

Consider, for instance, the act of observing an individual in a public space. As we watch someone go about their day, facing their own challenges and triumphs, it becomes a window into a different world. This simple act of observation can be a powerful catalyst for introspection. We begin to realize that everyone carries their burdens, dreams, and complexities. It prompts us to reevaluate our struggles and successes, fostering a sense of empathy and humility.

Observation allows us to appreciate the diversity of human experiences. It highlights that, despite our unique journeys, there are common threads that connect us all. This newfound awareness can be transformative, prompting us to be more appreciative of what we have. The success, challenges, and relationships that shape our lives take on new significance when viewed in the context of a broader human experience.

Moreover, observing others can inspire a sense of gratitude. It serves as a reminder that, in the grand scheme of things, our problems may not be as insurmountable as they seem. The struggles of others shed light on the resilience of the human spirit, encouraging us to approach our challenges with a renewed sense of determination. This shift in perspective can be a catalyst for personal growth, motivating us to strive for continuous improvement.

In essence, the power of observation lies in its ability to jolt us out of our self-focused narratives. It encourages a shift from a narrow, individualistic viewpoint to a more expansive and interconnected understanding of the world. By appreciating the struggles and successes of those around us, we gain a deeper appreciation for our own lives. The act of observation becomes a pathway to self-improvement, inspiring us to be more compassionate, grateful, and motivated in our pursuit of a more meaningful existence.

Empathy Vs Sympathy

Empathy and sympathy are often used interchangeably, but they represent distinct facets of human connection, each carrying its unique implications for understanding and supporting others. Delving into the nuances of empathy versus sympathy unveils the richness of these emotional responses, highlighting the crucial differences that shape the dynamics of our relationships.

EMPATHY:

Empathy is a profound and complex emotional response that involves the ability to fully understand and share the feelings of another person. It transcends mere recognition of someone's emotions; it requires us to step into their shoes, experiencing their joys, sorrows, and challenges as if they were our own. Empathy is an active and engaged process that demands both cognitive and emotional involvement. It involves listening attentively, discerning non-verbal cues, and being fully present with the other person.

One of the distinctive features of empathy is its transformative power in building connections and fostering a deeper understanding between individuals. When we empathize with someone, we validate their experiences, acknowledging the validity of their emotions. This shared connection often results in a heightened sense of compassion and support, creating a foundation for meaningful relationships. Empathy encourages open communication and helps break down emotional barriers, fostering an environment where people feel seen, heard, and understood.

Sympathy:

On the other hand, sympathy involves a more detached response to another person's emotions. While sympathy demonstrates a genuine concern for someone's well-being, it doesn't necessarily entail the same level of emotional immersion as empathy. Sympathy is often expressed through expressions of care, comfort, or consolation, conveying a sense of understanding without necessarily sharing in the depth of the other person's emotional experience.

Sympathy is characterized by a compassionate response to someone else's situation, providing solace and support without the complete emotional resonance that empathy entails. It acknowledges the other person's emotions from an external standpoint, offering comfort and kindness without necessarily entering into the emotional landscape they are navigating.

UNDERSTANDING WHEN to express empathy versus sympathy is a nuanced aspect of emotional intelligence that significantly impacts the quality of our interactions and relationships. These two responses, while both rooted in compassion, are distinct and are most effective in different contexts.

When to Show Empathy:

Empathy is particularly potent in situations where a deep, emotional understanding is required. When someone is going through a challenging experience or expressing intense emotions, offering empathy means actively connecting with their feelings. This involves not only acknowledging their emotional state but also making a concerted effort to comprehend the intricacies of their experience. It's about sharing in their joy, sorrow, or struggle on a profound level.

Empathy is especially valuable in interpersonal conflicts, grief, or moments of vulnerability. By expressing empathy, we signal to the other person that we are fully present, ready to listen without judgment, and willing to share in their emotional journey. This kind of response fosters trust, strengthens bonds, and creates a supportive environment where individuals feel genuinely seen and understood.

When to Show Sympathy:

Sympathy, on the other hand, is often more appropriate in situations where a degree of emotional distance is necessary or when understanding the intricate details of someone's experience may be challenging. Sympathy allows us to convey compassion and concern without necessarily immersing ourselves fully in the emotional landscape of the other person.

For instance, sympathy is often expressed in cases of loss, illness, or general hardships where we may not be able to fully comprehend the depth of someone's emotions. Offering sympathy involves acknowledging their pain, extending kindness, and providing support, but without necessarily attempting to step into their shoes.

<u>Caring</u>

Caring, as a profound and multifaceted noun, encapsulates the essence of compassion, concern, and genuine interest in the well-being of oneself and others. This intrinsic human quality has the remarkable capacity to catalyze personal growth, shaping individuals into empathetic, resilient, and socially aware beings. The impact of caring is particularly profound in the nurturing environments provided by parents or guardians, whose acts of care become the foundation for a lifetime of emotional and personal development.

At its core, caring involves a deep commitment to the welfare and happiness of others. This can manifest in various forms, from the physical and tangible aspects of nurturing to the intangible realms of emotional support and understanding. The acts of care we experience in our formative years, especially from parents or guardians, lay the groundwork for our perception of self, others, and the world.

Parents or guardians, as primary caregivers, play a pivotal role in shaping our understanding of caring from the earliest stages of life. The provision of basic needs, such as food, shelter, and safety, forms the foundational layer of care. This physical caregiving is crucial for an individual's survival and healthy development. It establishes a sense of security and trust, creating a stable environment where emotional and intellectual growth can take root.

Beyond meeting basic needs, caring takes on a transformative role in shaping emotional intelligence and resilience. Parents or guardians who offer emotional support, listen attentively, and provide comfort during times of distress contribute significantly to the development of a child's emotional well-being. These acts of caring foster a secure attachment, enhancing a child's capacity for forming healthy relationships and navigating the complexities of social interactions.

Moreover, witnessing and experiencing caring behaviors at a young age establishes a powerful template for how individuals perceive their roles in relationships and society. Children who grow up in environments characterized by love, empathy, and consistent care are more likely to internalize these values. As they mature, this internalized sense of caring becomes a guiding principle for their actions, influencing how they treat others and approach challenges.

The impact of caring extends beyond childhood into adulthood, where individuals who have experienced genuine care are often more resilient, empathetic, and capable of forming meaningful connections.

The lessons learned from the caring acts of parents or guardians become embedded in one's character, influencing decision-making, problem-solving, and overall well-being.

In essence, caring is a dynamic force that transcends the immediate moment of need. It is a lifelong companion that shapes our character, influences our relationships, and fosters personal growth. The acts of care bestowed upon us by our parents or guardians not only meet our physical and emotional needs but also contribute to the development of a well-rounded and compassionate individual, laying the groundwork for a lifetime of meaningful connections and personal fulfillment.

When we take care of something we not only help the thing we are taking care of, but are growing alongside it as we learn from the experience and how it can help us have a better understanding of other people's wants and needs. Here are some examples of how taking care of something can assist us in becoming a better person.

1. Caring for Children:

Babysitting or caring for children offers a firsthand experience in understanding the intricate world of childhood. This responsibility requires patience, creativity, and adaptability as caregivers navigate the unique thought processes and emotional landscapes of young minds. The challenges and joys of childcare cultivate qualities such as empathy, communication skills, and the ability to respond to dynamic situations, all of which contribute to personal growth and a deeper understanding of human development.

2. Caring for Animals:

Taking care of animals involves a commitment to their well-being, requiring structured routines and patience. The responsibility of ensuring an animal's physical health, emotional comfort, and overall welfare fosters discipline and empathy. The unconditional love and companionship received from pets create an environment where individuals learn about the significance of nurturing bonds, responsibility, and the rewards of selfless care.

3. CARING FOR A GARDEN:

Nurturing a garden is a unique form of caregiving that connects individuals with the cycles of growth, patience, and the beauty of the natural world. The act of tending to plants demands dedication, consistent effort, and an understanding of the needs of different species. As the garden flourishes, individuals experience the satisfaction of hard work, learn about the importance of perseverance, and develop a profound appreciation for the interconnectedness of life.

4. Caring for Elderly Family Members:

Assuming the role of a caregiver for elderly family members is a responsibility that involves compassion, patience, and an understanding of the aging process. Providing physical and emotional support to the elderly fosters empathy, resilience, and a heightened awareness of the unique challenges faced by aging individuals. This form of caregiving also deepens interpersonal connections and instills a sense of gratitude for the wisdom and experiences of older generations.

5. Caring for the Environment:

Environmental stewardship is a form of caring that extends beyond individual relationships to encompass the well-being of the planet. Activities such as recycling, reducing waste, and sustainable practices contribute to a sense of global responsibility. Caring for the environment instills values of conservation, mindfulness, and a recognition of the impact of individual actions on the broader ecosystem.

It is easy to go through life thinking of only ourselves. Our instincts try and make it that way as a safety and survival mechanism, but understanding the point of view of another and observing how your life truly differs from other individuals awakens a new perspective on life and how we should lead. From observing people's day-to-day lives to taking care of individuals or things to learning their wants and needs helps us understand ourselves and the way everyone thinks and acts differently which ultimately makes us better.

Chapter 11: Knowledge and Wisdom

In the intricate tapestry of human existence, knowledge and wisdom stand as the cornerstones that elevate individuals to the pinnacle of personal development. These two symbiotic components, intertwined yet distinct, weave a narrative of continual self-improvement and enlightenment. Embracing knowledge is akin to acquiring the tools, and wisdom is the artistry that guides their adept usage. Together, they forge a path toward becoming a better person, facilitating not only individual growth but also fostering positive impacts on society.

Knowledge, the accumulation of information and skills, serves as the fuel for personal advancement. It acts as a catalyst, empowering individuals to navigate the complexities of life with confidence and competence. For instance, in the professional realm, possessing a deep well of knowledge in a specific field can open doors to career opportunities. Employers seek individuals who are not just competent but also knowledgeable, recognizing the inherent value of a well-informed mind.

Moreover, knowledge acts as a beacon, illuminating the path toward understanding diverse perspectives and fostering empathy. In an interconnected world, being aware of different cultures, histories, and viewpoints is paramount. A knowledgeable person possesses the capacity to engage in meaningful conversations, bridging gaps and promoting harmony. By understanding the intricacies of global issues, one can contribute meaningfully to discussions, ultimately participating in the collective pursuit of solutions.

However, knowledge alone can be likened to raw materials awaiting transformation. It is the application of wisdom that molds this knowledge into a force for good. Wisdom is the nuanced ability to discern, judge, and act with prudence. Unlike knowledge, which is often associated with facts and information, wisdom draws from experience, reflection, and an understanding of the broader context.

Wisdom manifests in decision-making, problem-solving, and ethical considerations. A person endowed with wisdom possesses the discernment to navigate moral dilemmas, weighing the consequences of their actions on themselves and others. In interpersonal relationships, wisdom enables effective communication, conflict resolution, and the cultivation of meaningful connections. It is the glue that binds knowledge with ethical conduct, fostering a sense of responsibility and contributing to the creation of a harmonious society.

The synergy between knowledge and wisdom becomes most evident when individuals actively seek to apply their understanding to real-world scenarios. For instance, a person knowledgeable about sustainable practices may use their wisdom to implement eco-friendly choices in their daily life, contributing to the broader environmental cause. In this way, the combination of knowledge and wisdom transforms information into action, creating a positive ripple effect that extends beyond individual growth to societal betterment.

Knowledge and Wisdom go hand in hand on the key component to synergize with all factors within the book. With these two components, there isn't anything you can accomplish by gaining these traits.

Learning from Others

One of the most enriching and efficient ways to broaden one's understanding of the world is by tapping into the collective wisdom of others. Learning from those who have walked diverse paths, faced unique challenges, and accumulated a wealth of insights offers an invaluable shortcut to personal growth and enlightenment.

At the heart of gaining knowledge and wisdom from others lies the art of active listening. When engaging in conversations, whether with mentors, peers, or experts in a given field, attentive listening is the gateway to understanding. It involves more than just hearing words; it requires a genuine openness to absorb information, an empathetic connection with the speaker, and a willingness to suspend preconceived notions. Through active listening, one can glean not only factual information but also the nuances of experience and the wisdom embedded in personal narratives.

Mentorship emerges as a powerful conduit for knowledge transfer. Seeking guidance from those who have traversed similar paths or excelled in areas of interest provides a shortcut to success. Mentors offer a unique blend of experience-based insights, practical advice, and emotional support. By cultivating mentor-mentee relationships, individuals can tap into a wellspring of knowledge, learning not only from the mentor's triumphs but also from their mistakes and the invaluable lessons embedded within them.

This can also act as a way of using your relationships to better help yourself and grow a stronger bond from the individual for those you admire and their way of doing things.

In addition to mentorship, the diverse perspectives of peers contribute significantly to one's learning journey. Engaging in meaningful conversations with individuals from different backgrounds, cultures, and professions widens the scope of understanding. This cultural exchange fosters the cross-pollination of ideas, challenging assumptions, and nurturing a more holistic view of the world. Collaborative learning environments, such as study groups or professional networks, provide fertile ground for the cultivation of knowledge and wisdom through collective exploration and shared experiences. Every voice has a story and from it, you can learn better ways of finding your pathway and learning from their mistakes or gaining from their triumphs.

Beyond personal interactions, the written and spoken works of scholars, philosophers, and thought leaders serve as timeless repositories of wisdom. Books, podcasts, lectures, and documentaries are rich resources that offer insights into diverse subjects. By immersing oneself in these mediums, individuals can benefit from the distilled knowledge and perspectives of experts, gaining a deeper understanding of complex topics and acquiring the tools needed for critical thinking. Online courses, tutorial videos, and even an easy car ride podcast, while you're out, can help improve you on topics and things that you would have never known and make you more well-rounded and knowledgeable on topics.

Moreover, the digital age has ushered in unprecedented access to information through online courses, webinars, and educational platforms. Leveraging these resources enables individuals to learn from experts worldwide, breaking down geographical barriers and democratizing education. The ability to choose from a plethora of subjects and learning formats empowers individuals to tailor their learning experiences, aligning them with personal interests and goals. There are worries about not being able to afford schooling, but a lot of schools now offer free online courses as well as the sources and materials from their classes. You can read and take tests on topics without even attending or paying a single dime while gaining the knowledge you want to learn.

<u>Learning from our Own Mistakes</u>

The lessons gleaned from our own experiences stand as profound catalysts for growth. The crucible of life presents a myriad of challenges, failures, and triumphs, each contributing to the intricate mosaic of who we are. While successes bring joy, it is in the crucible of our mistakes and failures that the true alchemy of personal transformation occurs. These experiences, far from being setbacks, serve as stepping stones toward a more resilient, insightful, and self-aware version of ourselves.

Failures, often stigmatized in society, are, in reality, invaluable tutors on the path to self-improvement. Each misstep is a silent mentor, guiding us toward a deeper understanding of our strengths and weaknesses. For instance, consider the classic scenario of academic setbacks. Failing to meet a deadline or scoring poorly on an exam can be disheartening, but these experiences underscore the importance of time management, effective study habits, and seeking help when needed. The sting of failure becomes a beacon, illuminating areas for improvement and instilling the resilience needed to navigate future challenges.

Mistakes, viewed through the lens of learning, become a blueprint for progress. In the professional realm, a project gone awry or a business decision leading to adverse consequences can be disheartening. However, these missteps offer a wealth of insights. They prompt a reassessment of strategies, a refinement of skills, and a recalibration of approaches. In the crucible of our professional endeavors, mistakes serve as touchpoints for growth, offering the raw material from which innovation and success can emerge.

Moreover, personal relationships serve as a fertile ground for self-discovery through experiences. Miscommunications, conflicts, and lapses in judgment can strain connections, but they also illuminate the dynamics of human interaction. Each interpersonal stumble provides an opportunity for reflection, fostering emotional intelligence, and enhancing communication skills. By learning from our relational missteps, we cultivate empathy, patience, and a deeper understanding of the intricacies of human connection.

Reflecting on one's experiences also unveils the power of perspective. What might seem like a colossal failure at the moment often transforms into a pivotal point of growth when viewed through the lens of time and reflection. Consider the example of an individual who faced rejection in a job application.

While initially disheartening, this setback may lead to a subsequent opportunity that aligns more closely with their passions and strengths. The ability to extract lessons from such experiences grants us the resilience to face future uncertainties with a renewed sense of purpose and determination.

In the realm of personal habits and lifestyle choices, errors also serve as potent educators. Whether it's neglecting one's health, procrastinating on important tasks, or succumbing to negative patterns of behavior, each misstep carries within it the seeds of transformation. Recognizing these patterns prompts a commitment to self-improvement. For instance, adopting healthier lifestyle choices or cultivating discipline in daily routines becomes a conscious effort to learn from past mistakes and pave the way for a more balanced and fulfilling life.

Never forget that we may fall down sometimes, but we all get back up and move on. Don't let these hard times weigh you down and know that it only takes that single step to get the ball rolling and the gears turning. Try and try again no matter how many times you fail as long as you learn from your failures you will grow and gain the ability to move on.

Using our Gained Knowledge and Wisdom

The wealth of knowledge and wisdom acquired throughout our lives is a versatile and invaluable asset, capable of enriching every facet of our existence. This repository of understanding, gleaned from experiences, learning, and the wisdom of others, has the power to elevate our relationships, amplify our professional endeavors, enhance our hobbies, fortify our finances, and transcend the boundaries of personal growth.

In the realm of relationships, the application of acquired wisdom fosters deeper connections and empathy. Understanding the intricacies of effective communication, conflict resolution, and emotional intelligence nurtures healthier bonds with friends, family, and romantic partners. Knowledge of diverse perspectives and cultural sensitivity cultivates an inclusive mindset, enriching the tapestry of our social interactions. The ability to draw from experiences and empathize with others' journeys forms the bedrock of meaningful connections, creating a network of support and understanding.

PROFESSIONALLY, THE amalgamation of knowledge and wisdom is a potent formula for success. In the dynamic landscape of the workplace, a well-informed mind can adapt to challenges and seize opportunities. Continuous learning and a wise application of skills enable individuals to navigate the complexities of their chosen fields, positioning them as assets within their professional ecosystems. Wisdom in decision-making, leadership, and interpersonal dynamics elevates not only individual career trajectories but also contributes to the collective success of teams and organizations.

Hobbies, often seen as personal pursuits, are also enriched by the infusion of knowledge and wisdom. Whether it's cultivating a passion for art, sports, or music, a deeper understanding enhances the enjoyment and mastery of these activities. For instance, a well-informed artist can draw inspiration from diverse artistic movements, and a wise musician can infuse emotion and nuance into their compositions. The pursuit of knowledge in hobbies becomes a lifelong journey, transforming leisure activities into avenues for personal expression and continuous self-discovery.

Financial literacy, another crucial aspect of life, is profoundly impacted by knowledge and wisdom. Understanding financial markets, budgeting, and investment strategies empowers individuals to make informed decisions about their money. Wise financial choices, informed by a comprehensive understanding of economic principles, lead to stability and long-term prosperity. The ability to navigate the intricacies of personal finance ensures that individuals can meet their financial goals and weather the inevitable uncertainties of economic landscapes.

Furthermore, the application of knowledge and wisdom extends to health and well-being. Informed lifestyle choices, nutrition, and exercise routines contribute to physical vitality and mental resilience. The wisdom to prioritize self-care and balance amidst life's demands enhances overall well-being, fostering a harmonious relationship between the body and mind.

The expansive influence of knowledge and wisdom extends across various domains of our lives. From nurturing relationships and excelling in professional pursuits to enhancing hobbies, fortifying finances, and prioritizing well-being, the informed and wise application of acquired insights transforms each aspect of our existence. Embracing the continuous journey of learning and growth ensures that the treasure trove of knowledge and wisdom becomes a guiding compass, navigating us toward a more enriched and purposeful life.

<u>Out of our Comfort Zone</u>

In the cocoon of our comfort zones, familiarity provides solace, routine offers security, and the known becomes a refuge from the uncertainties of the unknown. However, the paradox of personal growth lies in the revelation that true wisdom and knowledge often reside beyond the boundaries of comfort. Stepping out of the well-trodden paths of familiarity is an essential journey—one fraught with difficulties, but ultimately a transformative odyssey toward enlightenment.

The first hurdle in venturing beyond our comfort zones lies in the fear of the unknown. It's human nature to seek stability, and the prospect of stepping into uncharted territories triggers anxiety. The comfort zone, characterized by routine and predictability, may seem like a safe harbor, but in reality, it can become a stagnant pond, stifling personal and intellectual growth. The difficulty lies not just in the act of stepping out but in overcoming the inertia that holds us captive within the familiar.

Learning, by its nature, is a challenging process. Acquiring new skills, assimilating unfamiliar information, and adapting to novel perspectives requires effort and perseverance. The discomfort associated with grappling with the unknown can be daunting, leading many to retreat to the perceived safety of what is already known. The fear of failure, the struggle to understand complex concepts, and the initial awkwardness of unfamiliar tasks contribute to the discomfort of learning. However, it is precisely within these challenges that the seeds of knowledge and wisdom find fertile ground.

Venturing beyond the comfort zone fosters resilience and adaptability. Consider, for example, the individual who decides to learn a new language. Initially, the process might be riddled with uncertainty, stumbling over pronunciation, and grappling with unfamiliar grammatical structures. However, as the learner persists, the brain adapts, creating new neural connections and linguistic frameworks. The discomfort of the initial learning phase transforms into linguistic proficiency, opening doors to new cultures, perspectives, and avenues for communication.

───────────

MOREOVER, THE DISCOMFORT of learning extends to interpersonal dynamics. Engaging with individuals from diverse backgrounds, with contrasting opinions and experiences, challenges preconceived notions and fosters intellectual growth. It requires humility to acknowledge gaps in understanding and the wisdom to embrace perspectives that differ from our own. The discomfort of navigating these intellectual crossroads paves the way for a more nuanced worldview and a deeper understanding of the complexities inherent in human interactions.

The process of stepping out of the comfort zone also confronts us with the risk of failure. Failure, however, is not a dead end but a detour on the road to success. Each setback, each stumble, provides valuable insights and lessons. For instance, in the professional realm, taking on challenging projects or assuming leadership roles may seem daunting, but the experiential learning that accompanies these endeavors shapes leaders and innovators. The discomfort of grappling with uncertainties becomes a crucible for resilience, problem-solving, and strategic thinking.

In the long run, the difficulties encountered in the pursuit of knowledge and wisdom become the very building blocks of personal growth. The discomfort of learning reshapes our cognitive landscape, fostering adaptability, resilience, and a heightened capacity for understanding. Beyond the immediate challenges lies a reservoir of knowledge and wisdom that transforms individuals into lifelong learners, capable of navigating the complexities of an ever-evolving world.

We get stronger when we learn from our mistakes. Messing up isn't a dead-end; it's like a guide telling us how to do better. Every time we goof up, it's a chance to figure out what went wrong and get smarter. Facing problems, especially the ones we create ourselves, makes us think about things, adjust, and come out tougher. Learning from our mistakes helps us handle tough situations, deal with uncertainties, and move forward in life, becoming better versions of ourselves. With the knowledge and wisdom we gain from others, from ourselves, and the tools we use we will be better and ultimately, do better.

Chapter 12: Peace of Mind

From the dawn of consciousness, humans have grappled with the profound question of their existence, yearning to unravel the mysteries that define the very essence of life. This innate curiosity has driven individuals and civilizations to embark on a relentless quest for the ultimate answers, a journey marked by philosophical inquiries, scientific exploration, and spiritual introspection. In this exploration, humans seek to decipher the purpose of their existence and unravel the intricacies of why they are here on this cosmic journey.

One avenue through which humans strive for ultimate answers is philosophy, the discipline that delves into the fundamental nature of existence, reality, and knowledge. Philosophers throughout history have grappled with the enigma of human purpose, debating questions that transcend time and culture. Some philosophers contemplated the inherent meaninglessness of existence, challenging individuals to create their own purpose in a seemingly indifferent universe.

Moreover, moral and ethical philosophies have emerged as frameworks to guide individuals in their quest for a meaningful life. The pursuit of virtues and the examination of ethical principles offer a compass to navigate the complexities of human existence, prompting individuals to contribute positively to society and cultivate a sense of purpose through their actions.

Parallel to philosophical exploration, the scientific method has been a powerful tool in humanity's pursuit of ultimate answers. Scientific inquiry seeks to comprehend the laws governing the cosmos, the origins of life, and the intricacies of human consciousness. Through disciplines such as cosmology, biology, and neuroscience, scientists strive to uncover the underlying principles that govern existence.

The quest for answers has led to groundbreaking discoveries, revealing the awe-inspiring complexity of the universe and the interconnectedness of all life. While science provides a methodical and empirical approach to understanding the world, it raises new questions about the purpose of consciousness and the role humans play in the grand tapestry of existence.

IN ADDITION TO PHILOSOPHY and science, spirituality and religious traditions offer a profound avenue for individuals to seek ultimate answers to life's mysteries. Across cultures, religions provide frameworks that offer explanations for the purpose of human existence and prescribe ways to live a purposeful life. Whether through prayer, meditation, or ritual, spiritual practices provide individuals with a means to connect with a higher power and find solace in the face of existential uncertainties.

These spiritual traditions often impart moral and ethical guidance, fostering a sense of community and shared purpose among believers. The quest for spiritual enlightenment becomes a personal journey, as individuals seek to align themselves with a higher purpose and transcend the mundane aspects of everyday life.

The human quest for ultimate answers to life's fundamental questions is a multifaceted journey, encompassing philosophy, science, and spirituality. From the existential inquiries of philosophers to the empirical investigations of scientists and the spiritual reflections of individuals, humanity's pursuit of purpose and meaning is an enduring testament to the depth of human curiosity. But how does this affect us on a personal level? We are looking for something that makes us feel whole or content in our lives to our greatest questions. Why am I here? Why was I born this way? What should I do? With these great questions, we must look inward and seek a journey of self-discovery by unlocking what makes us who we are and what our goal is in life.

<u>Who am I?</u>

In the labyrinth of self-discovery, humans grapple with the profound and perennial question, "Who am I?" This existential inquiry goes beyond the surface of our existence, delving into the intricate layers of identity that shape our perception of self and how others perceive us. The quest to unravel the complexities of our being involves a dynamic interplay of introspection, external perspectives, strengths, weaknesses, and the unique amalgamation of personality traits and quirks that make each individual's answer to this question as fluid as life itself.

AT THE CORE OF THE quest for self-understanding lies the introspective journey, where individuals confront their innermost thoughts, emotions, and beliefs. Our self-perception is often shaped by personal experiences, cultural influences, and the narrative we construct about our own lives. As we navigate the tapestry of memories, aspirations, and fears, we sift through the various roles we play – son or daughter, friend or colleague – attempting to distill a cohesive sense of self.

Yet, the self we perceive is not a static entity but an evolving construct, influenced by the ebb and flow of life's experiences. Strengths and weaknesses become integral facets of this self-perception, acting as mirrors that reflect the multifaceted nature of our identity. Acknowledging strengths can bolster confidence while confronting weaknesses becomes an opportunity for growth and self-improvement.

Simultaneously, our identity is shaped by the reflections we find in the mirrors of others – the perceptions, expectations, and judgments that society and individuals cast upon us. The interplay between how we see ourselves and how others see us creates a dynamic tension that further complicates the answer to the question of identity. Social roles, relationships, and societal norms influence the external facets of our identity, shaping the roles we inhabit and the masks we wear in different contexts.

While external perspectives can provide valuable insights, they can also limit our understanding of ourselves. The challenge lies in navigating the balance between authentic self-expression and societal expectations, as individuals strive to embrace their uniqueness while conforming to the norms that govern their communities.

Within the intricate tapestry of identity, strengths and weaknesses emerge as pivotal threads. Strengths, whether innate talents or cultivated skills contribute to our sense of competence and purpose. These attributes often define our achievements, shaping the narrative of our lives. Conversely, weaknesses, vulnerabilities, and limitations we grapple with provide opportunities for humility, resilience, and growth.

The dance between strengths and weaknesses forms the yin and yang of our identity, creating a delicate equilibrium that defines our character. It is in embracing the entirety of our being – the strengths that propel us forward and the weaknesses that ground us – that we find a more authentic answer to the question of who we are.

Adding vibrant hues to the canvas of identity are the unique personality traits and quirks that make each individual a distinct expression of humanity. Whether introverted or extroverted, analytical or creative, serious or whimsical, these qualities contribute to the richness of our identity. Our quirks, the idiosyncrasies that set us apart, become the brushstrokes that paint the portrait of our individuality.

<u>Why am I Here?</u>

the question of why we are here echoes through the corridors of our minds, compelling us to seek meaning and purpose in our lives. The innate human desire for purpose is deeply intertwined with the need to validate our actions, to find significance in the seemingly chaotic dance of existence. This quest for purpose serves as a guiding light, a compass that directs our choices, actions, and aspirations, as we yearn for confirmation that we are indeed on a path that aligns with our understanding of why we are here.

The need for purpose stems from a fundamental human drive to make sense of our existence and to imbue our lives with significance. Purpose provides a framework for understanding the meaning behind our actions, the relationships we cultivate, and the goals we pursue. It is the glue that binds together the disparate elements of our lives, offering a sense of direction and coherence in the face of life's uncertainties.

As social beings, we seek validation and acknowledgment from our peers and society at large. Purpose becomes a tool for self-validation, a means to measure the impact of our contributions and the value we bring to the world. This validation, in turn, reinforces our sense of self-worth and provides a foundation for a fulfilling and meaningful life.

The notion of purpose is inherently individualized, varying from person to person based on a myriad of factors such as personal values, cultural influences, and life experiences. What constitutes a meaningful purpose for one person may differ radically for another. This individualization adds a nuanced layer to the exploration of why we are here, recognizing that the kaleidoscope of human existence is painted with diverse hues of purpose.

Furthermore, the purpose of our lives is not a static concept but a dynamic and evolving force. As we journey through the stages of life, our priorities, values, and aspirations transform.

The purpose that fuels our passions in youth may shift as we navigate the complexities of adulthood, and further transform in the reflective years of later life. Each stage brings new challenges and opportunities, prompting a reevaluation of our purpose and a recalibration of our life's trajectory.

The ever-changing nature of purpose invites individuals to engage in continual self-reflection, adapting their sense of meaning to align with the evolving contours of their lives. This adaptability allows for resilience in the face of adversity and fosters a capacity to find purpose even amid life's unpredictable twists and turns.

Centering Ourselves

As we navigate the complexities of existence, the need to center ourselves becomes essential for maintaining mental well-being and finding answers to life's most profound questions. Embracing practices that foster mindfulness, self-reflection, and connection with our inner selves can be instrumental in cultivating a sense of tranquility and purpose.

One of the cornerstone practices for centering oneself is mindfulness meditation. By immersing oneself in the present moment, individuals can quiet the noise of external distractions and cultivate a heightened awareness of their thoughts and emotions. Mindfulness meditation encourages a non-judgmental observation of the present, allowing for a deep connection with the core of one's being. Techniques such as focused breathing, body scan meditations, and guided mindfulness exercises can serve as powerful tools to anchor the mind and foster inner peace.

Mindfulness practices not only alleviate stress but also create a space for self-discovery, enabling individuals to explore their values, desires, and intrinsic motivations. This self-awareness lays the foundation for uncovering a sense of purpose and clarity amidst life's uncertainties.

Engaging in regular self-reflection is another potent method for centering ourselves and navigating life's big questions. Taking time for introspection allows individuals to examine their beliefs, aspirations, and fears. Journaling, in particular, provides a tangible outlet for expressing thoughts and emotions, facilitating a deeper understanding of oneself.

BY DOCUMENTING DAILY experiences, reflections, and gratitude, individuals can trace patterns in their lives, identify areas of personal growth, and pinpoint sources of joy and fulfillment. This practice not only fosters a sense of inner peace but also serves as a compass for aligning one's actions with their values and purpose.

The natural world has a profound ability to evoke a sense of tranquility and interconnectedness. Spending time in nature, whether through walks in the park, hikes in the mountains, or moments of quiet contemplation by the ocean, can be a powerful practice for centering oneself. Nature provides a respite from the demands of modern life and offers a space for reflection and rejuvenation.

Observing the cycles of nature can also inspire contemplation on the cyclical nature of life, helping individuals find solace in the ebb and flow of their journeys. Whether it's the rustle of leaves in the wind or the rhythmic crashing of waves, these natural rhythms can serve as a reminder of the greater interconnectedness that binds all living things.

There are many techniques to centering ourselves, you just have to find the one that works for you and can help get you to that calm and reflective state. The idea of centering yourself is to let your mind wander yet focus on these self-reflections and self-discovery on the questions we have for ourselves and for the world we live in. We can not let these great questions of life become factors of our destruction and downfall. Some people get consumed by these questions and make it their all-time focus which can have inverse and negative effects on their lives. Sometimes it's even best to take a step back and live in the moment.

Living in the Moment

In the fast-paced rhythm of modern life, the concept of living in the moment has emerged as a profound antidote to the anxieties associated with an uncertain future. The fleeting nature of time underscores the importance of seizing each day with intention and gratitude. The wisdom encapsulated in the phrase "carpe diem" resonates as a powerful call to action, urging individuals to appreciate the present, reflect on their happiness, and break free from the constraints that hinder them from living life to the fullest.

Life's unpredictability is a stark reality that urges us to value the present moment. The future remains uncertain, filled with variables beyond our control. It is in this acknowledgment of life's impermanence that the invitation to live in the moment gains its significance. Every passing second is an opportunity to create lasting memories, forge meaningful connections, and pursue passions that bring joy and fulfillment.

Living in the moment is not merely a passive acceptance of the present but an active engagement with life's richness. It involves a conscious effort to appreciate the small joys, savor the experiences, and be fully present in each unfolding moment. Whether it's the warmth of a sunrise, the laughter shared with loved ones, or the simple pleasures of daily life, these moments collectively compose the fabric of our existence.

To make the most of every day requires a shift in perspective—an intentional focus on the quality of experiences rather than the quantity of time. It prompts individuals to prioritize what truly matters, to invest time in relationships, and to pursue activities that align with their values and bring a sense of purpose.

Living in the moment necessitates periodic reflection on one's own happiness. It involves an honest assessment of whether the current trajectory of life aligns with personal aspirations and values. The pursuit of happiness is not a distant destination but an ongoing journey, and self-reflection serves as a compass, guiding individuals toward choices that foster contentment and fulfillment.

Acknowledging and addressing negative or constricting influences is an integral part of this reflection process. Whether it's unfulfilling relationships, toxic environments, or self-imposed limitations, the pursuit of living in the moment requires the courage to confront and overcome obstacles that hinder authentic happiness. By doing so, individuals can liberate themselves from unnecessary burdens and open up space for more meaningful experiences.

Living in the moment also involves breaking free from the constraints that hold us back from fully embracing life. It requires a conscious effort to let go of worries about the future, regrets from the past, and self-imposed limitations that hinder personal growth. This liberation involves cultivating a mindset of acceptance and resilience, recognizing that challenges are inherent to the human experience but need not define our capacity for joy and fulfillment.

In essence, living in the moment is an active choice to be present, appreciate the beauty of life, and pursue happiness with a sense of urgency. By adopting a carpe diem philosophy, individuals can transform the ordinary into the extraordinary, finding fulfillment in the every day and creating a life rich in meaningful experiences.

The Sands of Time

The relentless march of time is an immutable force, an ever-present reminder of life's transience and the inevitability of change. As we navigate the ebb and flow of temporal currents, we confront a choice: to resist the passage of time, struggle against its current, or surrender, allowing the unfolding of moments with a graceful acceptance. Embracing the temporal journey requires a profound understanding of the nature of time and a willingness to let go of resistance in favor of going with the flow.

Time, as a fundamental dimension of our existence, operates as a continuous and irreversible force. Its steady progression shapes our experiences, molds our memories, and propels us through the various stages of life. Each tick of the clock represents a moment that becomes a part of our narrative, contributing to the intricate mosaic of our journeys.

In our complex relationship with time, it is not uncommon to find ourselves resisting its onward march. Faced with the inevitability of change, individuals may grapple with a sense of nostalgia or anxiety about an uncertain future. The struggle against time manifests in the desire to hold onto fleeting moments, to preserve the status quo, and to resist the alterations that time inevitably brings.

This resistance often stems from a fear of the unknown, the discomfort of stepping into uncharted territories, or the longing for the familiar. However, the attempt to resist time's flow can lead to a sense of stagnation, preventing personal growth and hindering the natural evolution of life.

Contrary to the resistance that characterizes the struggle against time, embracing the flow involves a conscious decision to let go of the need for absolute control. It is an acknowledgment that change is inherent in the very fabric of existence and that each passing moment is an opportunity for growth and renewal. Going with the flow requires cultivating a mindset of acceptance, resilience, and adaptability.

Letting go does not imply passivity; rather, it is an active engagement with the present moment and a surrender to the natural progression of time. It involves appreciating the beauty of impermanence and finding liberation in the acceptance of life's inherent dynamism. By relinquishing their grip on the past or anxieties about the future, individuals can navigate the currents of time with a sense of openness and curiosity.

Embracing the flow of time also entails a willingness to adapt to change. Life is a series of unfolding chapters, each bringing new experiences, challenges, and opportunities. Whether it's transitions in career, relationships, or personal identity, the ability to adapt allows individuals to navigate the river of time with greater ease.

Resisting change can lead to stagnation and a missed opportunity for personal and collective evolution. By embracing change, individuals not only open themselves up to new possibilities but also cultivate a resilience that enables them to navigate the inevitable ups and downs of life with greater grace and fortitude.

The point of this chapter is this, We all want the big questions answered and we can help towards that journey by using practices and techniques to get there, but we can not let it take over our lives and instead should embrace every day like it is our last. Go do things that you wish could do as you never know what may come. Never live a life or regrets and try your hardest for yourself to live in the moment and be centered within your mind. Doing all of this will ultimately make you be better.

Chapter 13: Grief

Grief is an intricate and profoundly human response to loss, a journey through the labyrinth of emotions that follows the departure of someone or something deeply cherished. It is an experience universal to the human condition, transcending culture, age, and background. At its core, grief is the emotional, psychological, and physical reaction to the absence of someone or something significant, be it the death of a loved one, the end of a relationship, the loss of a job, or even the dissolution of a dream.

This intricate process encompasses a spectrum of emotions, ranging from disbelief and denial to anger, bargaining, depression, and, ultimately, acceptance. As Elisabeth Kübler-Ross famously articulated in her model of the five stages of grief, individuals may not necessarily linearly traverse these stages, and the intensity and duration of each stage can vary widely from person to person. Grief is a dynamic and evolving phenomenon, often defying the boundaries of neat categorization.

One of the defining features of grief is its ability to manifest in multifaceted ways. The emotional landscape of grief is characterized by a rollercoaster of sentiments, with waves of sorrow, guilt, regret, and anger crashing against the shores of the grieving individual's consciousness. The experience is not static; it morphs and transforms, challenging the bereaved to confront and grapple with their emotions on a profound level. Grief demands an acknowledgment of pain, an acceptance of the new reality, and the gradual reconstruction of a life reshaped by loss.

Beyond the emotional turmoil, grief also takes a toll on the physical and psychological well-being of those mourning. Sleep disturbances, changes in appetite, fatigue, and a heightened susceptibility to illness are just a few of the physical manifestations of grief. The mind, too, is deeply impacted, as cognitive functions may be impaired, concentration becomes elusive, and decision-making becomes a monstrous task. The journey through grief is, in essence, a holistic recalibration of the self.

IN SOCIETAL TERMS, grief is often encountered with a discomforted silence or an urge to rush the bereaved through the process. However, it is essential to recognize that grief cannot be neatly packaged into a specific timeframe. Each individual traverses their path at their own pace, and the healing process is as unique as the relationship or entity lost. Empathy, compassion, and a willingness to accompany the grieving on their journey are crucial components of fostering a supportive environment.

Why do we Grief?

Why do we grieve? The answer lies in the very fabric of our humanity, woven with threads of attachment, love, and the inherent interconnectedness we share with others and the world around us. Grief is the visceral response to the rupture of these ties, a testament to the depth of our connections and the impact that loss has on the very essence of who we are.

At its core, grief is a natural and adaptive response to the absence of someone or something that holds significance in our lives. The intensity of grief mirrors the strength of the bond severed, whether it be the loss of a beloved family member, a dear friend, a pet, or even an aspect of one's identity. In acknowledging and experiencing grief, individuals recalibrate their understanding of the world, the self, and the relationships that define their existence.

Loss catapults individuals into uncharted emotional territories, prompting them to navigate through a myriad of feelings that encompass sorrow, anger, guilt, and a profound sense of emptiness. It is through this emotional tumult that individuals begin to grapple with the intricate tapestry of their connections, confronting the reality that life is transient and ever-changing. Grief, then, becomes a mechanism for introspection and growth, a crucible in which individuals forge a deeper understanding of themselves and the world.

The impact of loss on an individual is not confined to the emotional realm; it reverberates through every facet of their being. Psychologically, grief can instigate a profound reevaluation of one's identity and purpose, often leading to existential questioning and a search for meaning. The physical toll of grief is palpable, with symptoms ranging from disrupted sleep patterns and changes in appetite to heightened stress levels. The bereaved find themselves navigating an altered reality, where the landscape is defined by absence and the need for adaptation is paramount.

Furthermore, the journey through grief is not a solitary one. Loss can either fragment or strengthen the social fabric of an individual's life. While some may find solace and support in their network of friends and family, others may grapple with isolation and a sense of abandonment. The societal response to grief plays a pivotal role in shaping the individual's experience, influencing their ability to express their emotions, and facilitating the healing process.

<u>Types of Grief</u>

There are different types of grief with varying factors that come into play. Here are some examples of different griefs that individuals and groups may or have experienced.

Anticipatory Grief:

Anticipatory grief occurs when individuals experience the impending loss of a loved one due to a terminal illness or a prolonged, irreversible condition. This form of grief allows individuals to grapple with the impending void and begin the process of emotional preparation. While it does not diminish the intensity of sorrow upon the actual passing, it offers an opportunity for gradual adjustment. For example, a family caring for a relative with a terminal illness may undergo anticipatory grief as they witness the gradual decline of their loved one's health.

Complicated Grief:

Complicated grief, also known as prolonged grief disorder, is characterized by an extended and intense mourning period that significantly disrupts an individual's daily life. This type of grief may be triggered by factors such as the sudden and unexpected nature of a loss or unresolved emotions surrounding the death. An example could be the death of a close friend in a tragic accident, leaving the bereaved struggling to come to terms with the abrupt and unforeseen end of the relationship.

AMBIGUOUS LOSS:

Ambiguous loss occurs when individuals face a situation of uncertainty or lack of closure about the status of a loved one. This can manifest in cases of disappearances, kidnappings, or situations where physical presence is lost, but the person is not declared dead. Families of missing persons or those dealing with a loved one suffering from severe dementia may grapple with ambiguous loss, navigating the emotional complexities of not knowing the fate of their loved ones.

Disenfranchised Grief:

Disenfranchised grief refers to the sense of loss that is not openly acknowledged or socially supported. This may occur in situations such as the death of a pet, the end of a non-traditional relationship, or the loss of a job. Society may downplay the significance of these losses, leaving individuals to grieve in isolation. An example is the profound grief experienced by someone after the death of a cherished pet, where the depth of the emotional bond is not always understood or accepted by others.

Collective Grief:

Collective grief transcends individual experiences, encompassing the shared sorrow felt by communities, societies, or nations in the face of a widespread tragedy or loss. Natural disasters, acts of terrorism, or global pandemics evoke collective grief as communities grapple with the magnitude of shared suffering. An example is the global grief experienced during a traumatic event, where people worldwide faced loss, uncertainty, and collective mourning for the lives disrupted and lost.

Secondary Grief:

Secondary grief refers to the emotional response experienced by individuals who are indirectly affected by a primary loss. This could include friends, coworkers, or neighbors who, while not directly connected to the deceased, feel the ripple effects of the loss within their social or professional circles. For instance, colleagues at a workplace might experience secondary grief when a coworker passes away, impacting the dynamics of the entire team.

Chronic Grief:

Chronic grief is characterized by a persistent and prolonged state of mourning that extends over an extended period. Unlike normal grief, which tends to diminish with time, chronic grief remains intense and pervasive, often hindering the individual's ability to move forward. This type of grief can result from multiple losses or a single, exceptionally profound loss that continues to reverberate through an individual's life.

Inhibited Grief:

Inhibited grief occurs when individuals suppress or restrain their emotional reactions to a loss. This may be influenced by cultural expectations, societal norms, or personal coping mechanisms that discourage open expression of grief. Inhibited grief can have long-term consequences, potentially leading to unresolved emotions and complications in the mourning process.

Nostalgic Grief:

Nostalgic grief involves a longing for the past and a deep sense of yearning for what once was. This type of grief is often associated with the loss of a significant life phase, such as the end of a fulfilling chapter, retirement, or the departure of grown children from the family home. Individuals experiencing nostalgic grief may grapple with a mix of sadness and fondness for the memories associated with the bygone era.

Traumatic Grief:

Traumatic grief arises from losses that involve sudden, violent, or distressing circumstances, such as accidents, homicides, or suicides. The traumatic nature of the loss can complicate the grieving process, introducing elements of shock, intrusive thoughts, and a heightened sense of vulnerability. Individuals facing traumatic grief may require specialized support to navigate the emotional aftermath of such distressing events.

Delayed Grief:

Delayed grief refers to a postponed or deferred mourning process. In some cases, individuals may initially suppress their emotions or focus on practical matters, only to experience the full impact of grief at a later time. This delayed response can be triggered by events such as anniversaries, significant life milestones, or the removal of distractions that once helped to mask the pain.

Existential Grief:

Existential grief emerges from the contemplation of life's meaning, purpose, and the inevitable reality of mortality. It often accompanies philosophical reflections on existence, one's legacy, and the broader questions of human existence. This type of grief may be prompted by events such as a midlife crisis, a significant health scare, or a period of profound introspection.

Treating and Accepting Grief

Grief is an inevitable facet of the human experience, and while it may seem an insurmountable challenge, there are coping strategies and treatment approaches that can provide solace and support to those grappling with loss. Recognizing that grief is a natural process and an integral part of healing is crucial in establishing a foundation for effective coping.

Engaging in expressive writing can be a therapeutic outlet for processing emotions associated with grief. Encouraging individuals to journal their thoughts, memories, and feelings allows them to externalize their inner turmoil. This exercise provides a safe space for the expression of pain, anger, and even moments of joy associated with the memories of the lost loved one. The act of putting pen to paper can be a cathartic release, promoting a deeper understanding of one's emotions.

Participating in support groups offers individuals the opportunity to share their experiences with others who have faced similar losses. Whether in-person or online, these communities create a space for empathy, validation, and mutual understanding. Connecting with people who can relate to the intricacies of grief fosters a sense of belonging and diminishes the isolation often felt during mourning.

Incorporating mindfulness practices and meditation into daily routines can help individuals navigate the overwhelming emotions associated with grief. Mindfulness encourages a non-judgmental awareness of the present moment, allowing individuals to observe their thoughts and feelings without becoming entangled in them. This practice provides a reprieve from the intensity of grief, fostering a sense of calm and acceptance.

Art therapy provides an alternative form of expression for those struggling to articulate their emotions verbally. Creating art, whether through painting, drawing, or sculpture, allows individuals to channel their grief into a tangible and symbolic form. The creative process itself can be therapeutic, offering a means of self-discovery and emotional release.

Engaging in regular physical activity can have a profound impact on mental well-being. Exercise releases endorphins, which are known as "feel-good" hormones, and can alleviate symptoms of depression and anxiety associated with grief. Whether it's walking, jogging, yoga, or any form of physical activity, incorporating movement into daily routines contributes to overall emotional resilience.

Professional counseling and therapy provide a structured and supportive environment for individuals to explore their grief with the guidance of a trained therapist. Various therapeutic modalities, such as cognitive-behavioral therapy (CBT) or grief counseling, can help individuals reframe their thoughts, develop coping mechanisms, and navigate the complexities of mourning.

Creating rituals or memorials in honor of the deceased can be a meaningful way to commemorate their life. This could involve establishing an annual tradition, planting a memorial garden, or organizing a memorial service. These rituals provide a sense of connection and continuity, allowing individuals to celebrate the positive aspects of their relationship with the departed.

While these coping strategies and treatment approaches can offer substantial support, it is crucial to emphasize that grief is a natural and transformative process. Acceptance, the final stage of grief according to some models, involves coming to terms with the reality of the loss and integrating it into one's life. It does not signify forgetting or diminishing the significance of what was lost but rather finding a way to carry the memories forward while embracing the present and the potential for a renewed sense of purpose and joy. In learning to cope with and accept grief, individuals embark on a journey of healing, resilience, and self-discovery that is uniquely their own.

Chapter 14: Pride and Humility

Pride and humility exist as the dual forces propelling individuals along the path of success and personal growth. Pride serves as the driving engine, motivating individuals to set high standards, achieve goals, and celebrate accomplishments. It is the beacon of self-assurance that fuels determination and resilience in the face of challenges. However, unchecked pride can lead to stagnation and resistance to learning from mistakes. On the other hand, humility acts as the essential counterbalance, fostering a mindset of openness and receptivity to new ideas, feedback, and experiences. Embracing humility allows individuals to acknowledge their imperfections, learn from failures, and continuously evolve. Success, in its truest sense, emerges from the delicate interplay between pride and humility—a harmonious dance where pride propels us forward and humility keeps us grounded, ensuring a journey of perpetual growth and achievement.

Pride

Pride, in its essence, is the profound sense of satisfaction and fulfillment derived from one's achievements, efforts, and identity. It is the emotional cornerstone that underpins a positive self-concept and plays a pivotal role in shaping individual motivation and ambition. Taking pride in what one does is a powerful affirmation of self-worth and a recognition of the dedication and hard work invested in a particular endeavor. Whether it be personal accomplishments, professional achievements, or creative pursuits, embracing pride instills a deep sense of purpose and satisfaction that fuels continued commitment to excellence.

When individuals take pride in their work, it serves as a catalyst for excellence. The satisfaction derived from a job well done becomes a driving force, propelling individuals to strive for even greater heights. Pride acts as a motivational beacon, encouraging individuals to set ambitious goals, overcome obstacles, and pursue challenges with unwavering determination. This positive reinforcement loop fosters a sense of resilience, pushing individuals to persevere in the face of adversity and cultivate a mindset that sees opportunities in every setback.

Moreover, pride extends beyond individual accomplishment; it fosters a sense of community and belonging. When people take pride in their collective achievements, whether as part of a team or a larger social group, it creates bonds that strengthen the fabric of relationships. Shared pride builds a sense of unity, collaboration, and mutual support, creating an environment where individuals are not only motivated by personal success but also by the success of those around them. In this way, pride becomes a force that not only elevates the individual but also contributes to the collective well-being and progress of a community.

Furthermore, the act of taking pride in one's work is an acknowledgment of the value and significance of the contributions made. It instills a sense of purpose and meaning in daily endeavors, transforming routine tasks into meaningful expressions of personal and professional identity. When individuals take pride in their work, it becomes a source of personal fulfillment, aligning their actions with their values and aspirations. This alignment contributes to a positive self-image and fosters a healthy sense of self-esteem, which, in turn, has cascading effects on overall mental well-being.

Taking pride in what one does and in the achievements amassed is a powerful and positive force that fuels personal and collective growth. The intrinsic motivation derived from pride acts as a catalyst for continuous improvement, propelling individuals to strive for excellence and encouraging collaboration within communities. By recognizing and celebrating successes, individuals not only enhance their well-being but also contribute to the flourishing of the larger tapestry of human achievement and progress. In the final analysis, taking pride in one's endeavors is not only beneficial on an individual level but is also a cornerstone for building a thriving and interconnected society.

Careful though as being too prideful can result in negative effects. If you become too prideful it can be off-putting to others and fall under narcissistic behavior. Having too much pride can also stunt room for growth as you become too stubborn about accepting newer ideas and ways of doing things.

<u>Humility</u>

Humility, a virtue often undervalued in a society that praises individual achievement, is the quality of recognizing one's limitations, embracing a modest view of oneself, and acknowledging the contributions and perspectives of others. At its core, humility acts as a compass for personal growth, serving as a constant reminder that there is always room for improvement. It allows individuals to navigate the delicate balance between self-awareness and a willingness to learn, fostering an environment conducive to development and advancement.

Having a degree of humility is particularly beneficial as it opens the door to self-reflection and a genuine understanding of one's strengths and weaknesses. This self-awareness becomes a catalyst for improvement, motivating individuals to seek knowledge, learn from experiences, and refine their skills. Humility provides the foundation for a growth mindset—a belief that abilities and intelligence can be developed through dedication and hard work. In this way, humility becomes a driving force behind continuous learning and improvement.

Moreover, humility encourages individuals to recognize the interconnectedness of their achievements with the efforts of others. It promotes a collaborative spirit, acknowledging that success is often a collective endeavor. By appreciating the diverse perspectives and contributions of those around them, individuals can leverage the power of teamwork and shared expertise. Humility fosters a sense of gratitude, leading to stronger relationships and a deeper understanding of the value each person brings to the table.

However, it is crucial to note that while humility is a virtue, an excess of it can have adverse effects. Too much humility can lead to a lack of self-esteem, where individuals undermine their own worth and potential. Excessive humility may result in a reluctance to assert oneself, diminishing the drive to pursue ambitious goals or take on leadership roles. In extreme cases, it can foster a mindset of complacency, where individuals become hesitant to challenge the status quo or strive for better outcomes.

ADDITIONALLY, AN OVERDOSE of humility may inhibit the development of courage and resilience. The fear of failure and the desire to avoid standing out can stifle innovation and creative thinking. A healthy sense of confidence and self-assuredness is necessary for individuals to take risks, overcome challenges, and pursue growth opportunities. Striking the right balance between humility and self-confidence is essential for maintaining a mindset that encourages continuous improvement while also fostering the courage to step outside one's comfort zone.

The Duality

Taking pride in one's accomplishments and recognizing areas for humility are integral aspects of personal and professional development. Pride can be derived from various facets of life, such as achievements, personal growth, and contributions to the community. For instance, individuals can rightfully take pride in their professional accomplishments—completing a challenging project, earning a promotion, or mastering a new skill. Celebrating these achievements is essential for fostering a positive self-image and motivation. Pride in one's work can be a driving force, leading to increased job satisfaction and a sense of purpose.

Furthermore, personal growth and resilience in the face of challenges are also worthy sources of pride. Overcoming obstacles, whether they be personal struggles or professional setbacks, demonstrates strength and determination. Individuals can take pride in their ability to adapt, learn from experiences, and emerge stronger from adversity. This form of pride serves as a testament to one's character and capacity for growth.

However, it is equally crucial to practice humility in the face of accomplishments. Recognizing that there is always room for improvement is an essential aspect of personal and professional humility. For example, even after a successful project, a humble individual might reflect on the process, acknowledging that there are alternative approaches or areas where efficiency could be enhanced. Humility in the context of personal growth involves acknowledging that the journey is ongoing and that there is always more to learn and experience.

IN THE REALM OF RELATIONSHIPS, taking pride in supportive and nurturing connections is important. Healthy relationships, whether personal or professional, contribute significantly to one's well-being and success. Celebrating the positive impact one has on others and the reciprocal support received fosters a sense of community and shared achievement.

Conversely, practicing humility in relationships involves recognizing that no one is infallible. Humble individuals appreciate the perspectives and contributions of others, understanding that collaboration and teamwork are essential components of success. In a professional setting, this might involve seeking input from colleagues, valuing diverse viewpoints, and acknowledging that collective efforts often lead to superior outcomes.

In the pursuit of knowledge and intellectual growth, individuals can take pride in their expertise and the mastery of a subject. This pride can be a source of confidence and motivation to continue expanding one's knowledge. However, humility is crucial here as well. Acknowledging that knowledge is vast and ever-evolving encourages a humble approach to learning. Embracing the idea that there is always more to discover and remaining open to different perspectives cultivates a mindset of continuous learning.

The duality of pride and humility is a powerful force in shaping personal and professional development. Taking pride in accomplishments, growth, and meaningful connections is essential for maintaining a positive self-image and fostering motivation. Simultaneously, humility serves as a grounding force, encouraging individuals to recognize areas for improvement, appreciate the contributions of others, and maintain an openness to new ideas and experiences. Striking a balance between pride and humility creates a pathway for holistic and sustainable growth, where achievements are celebrated, and the pursuit of excellence is coupled with a genuine awareness of one's capacity for improvement.

Chapter 15: The Future

Planning for the future is a thoughtful and strategic endeavor that requires a combination of foresight, goal-setting, and adaptability. Here are key considerations for an individual looking to plan for a successful and fulfilling future:

Set Clear Goals:

Clearly define short-term and long-term goals. Whether they involve career aspirations, personal development, or financial milestones, having specific objectives provides a roadmap for your journey.

Financial Planning:

Cultivate a habit of financial responsibility. Budgeting, saving, and investing wisely contribute to long-term financial security. Emergency funds and retirement planning should be integral components of your financial strategy.

Continuous Learning:

Embrace a mindset of continuous learning. In a rapidly evolving world, acquiring new skills and staying informed about industry trends enhances adaptability and career prospects. Consider pursuing additional education or certifications.

Career Development:

Strategically plan your career trajectory. Set milestones, seek mentorship, and explore opportunities for advancement. Networking and building professional relationships can open doors to new possibilities.

Health and Wellness:

Prioritize physical and mental well-being. Adopt a healthy lifestyle through regular exercise, balanced nutrition, and sufficient rest. Investing in your health ensures sustained energy and resilience to face challenges.

Build a Support System:

Cultivate strong relationships with family, friends, and mentors. A supportive network provides emotional stability and valuable guidance during life's ups and downs.

Risk Management:

Acknowledge that uncertainty is inherent in life. Develop resilience by being prepared for unexpected challenges. This may include having insurance coverage, both for health and property, as well as contingency plans for various scenarios.

Balance Work and Life:

Strive for a balance between professional and personal life. While pursuing career ambitions, ensure time for hobbies, leisure, and spending quality moments with loved ones.

Adaptability:

Stay adaptable in the face of change. The ability to pivot and adjust plans as circumstances evolve is a crucial skill. Embrace new opportunities and be open to reevaluating goals based on changing priorities.

Regular Reflection:

Periodically reflect on your progress and reassess your goals. Adjustments may be necessary as circumstances, priorities, and aspirations evolve over time.

Legal and Estate Planning:

Consider legal aspects such as drafting a will, establishing power of attorney, and making decisions about healthcare directives. Planning for the future includes ensuring your affairs are in order for various life stages.

Cultivate a Positive Mindset:

Foster a positive and optimistic mindset. A positive outlook not only enhances your well-being but also influences how you approach challenges and setbacks.

In essence, effective future planning involves a holistic approach that encompasses personal, professional, and financial aspects of life. By setting clear goals, being adaptable, and prioritizing well-being, individuals can navigate the uncertainties of the future with confidence and purpose.

The Mirror

In the quiet moments of self-reflection, the mirror becomes a portal to traverse the vast landscapes of our personal history, our current reality, and the untapped realms of our future aspirations. The Mirror Exercise invites individuals to embark on a journey through time, gazing upon their own reflection as a conduit to reconnect with the echoes of their past, the nuances of their present, and the aspirations of their future selves.

Journeying into the Past:

As you stand before the mirror, the room fades away, and you find yourself transported to the days of your youth. The exercise begins by envisioning the person you once were perhaps a child full of curiosity and untamed dreams. Take in the details of your younger self, the innocence in your eyes, the untamed enthusiasm, and the quirks that made you uniquely you. What did you love? What made you mad? Embrace the memories, the passions, and the insecurities that shaped your formative years. This reflection allows a deeper understanding of the roots from which your present self has grown.

Confronting the Present:

As the journey through time progresses, the mirror becomes a reflective surface for the present moment. See yourself as you are now, acknowledging the experiences that have molded you, the challenges that have tested your resilience, and the triumphs that have adorned your path. Take note of the lines etched by laughter and the scars that tell stories of battles fought and overcome. Consider your current likes and dislikes, the passions that still burn brightly, and the dreams that have evolved. The present reflection is a canvas painted with the hues of experiences, presenting an unfiltered image of your essence.

Envisioning the Future:

With the past and present reflections etched in your mind, turn your gaze towards the future. Imagine the person you aspire to become, a vision shaped by your deepest desires, values, and aspirations. What goals do you seek to achieve? What qualities do you wish to cultivate? Envision the life you want to lead, the relationships you wish to nurture, and the impact you hope to make on the world. The mirror becomes a canvas for your dreams, allowing you to paint a picture of the person you are working towards becoming.

The Mirror Exercise serves as a powerful tool for self-discovery and personal development. It prompts individuals to embrace the full spectrum of their existence, fostering a deeper connection with their past, a clearer understanding of their present, and a vivid vision of their desired future. In the reflection of one's own eyes, lies the potential for growth, transformation, and the realization of one's truest self. As you step away from the mirror, carry with you the insights gained through this exercise, for they hold the key to unlocking the doors of self-discovery and personal evolution.

<u>Conclusion</u>

We talked about a lot in this book about what makes up a human and why we do the things we do. From a societal aspect down to what internally on what makes us tick. Our choices, actions, likes, and dislikes stem from many sources as well as our personalities and characteristics. The exercises in this book portray what can help right now, but life is dynamic and as time goes on and you begin to change more there may be some practices no longer suitable for what you may need.

The key factor of this book is still the same though; improving ourselves. Doing better and Being better to become the best version of yourself is what should be strived for, but why is that? Why would we put that extra effort in when we could take the easy way out? The answer is, there is none. You can choose the easy way, but nothing is done easily, and shortcuts taken have never turned out how you want them to. Time continues to move in this world and it's something we can not stop. One day you may wake up and notice that you have regrets of what could have been. We should strive for greatness and put in that extra effort because we owe that to ourselves and those who care for us. Don't ruin your chance at something because of fear and take life by the reigns. Put these practices to the test and don't give up. The journey will be difficult, but every day little by little it will get easier, and always remember this:

Do Better. Be Better.